DOCTOR

THE TRIBE OF GUM

DOCTOR WHO
THE SCRIPTS

THE TRIBE OF GUM
ANTHONY COBURN

EDITED BY JOHN McELROY

TITAN BOOKS

LONDON

DOCTOR WHO *THE SCRIPTS* : THE TRIBE OF GUM
ISBN 1 85286 012 X

Published by
Titan Books Ltd
58 St Giles High St
London WC2H 8LH

First edition January 1988
10 9 8 7 6 5 4 3 2 1

By arrangement with BBC Books, a division of BBC Enterprises Ltd

Typeset by Rapid Communications Ltd, London, WC1
Printed and bound in Great Britain by Cox and Wyman Ltd, Reading,
Berkshire

CONTENTS

INTRODUCTION

Welcome to the first in what we plan to make a long series of *Doctor Who* script books.

It is now twenty-four years since the first episode of *Doctor Who* appeared on British television screens. During this time the programme has become a popular success world-wide. Much has been written about the origins of *Doctor Who*. A lot of the details have been lost in the mists of time, and frequently people's memories of the early days are patchy. The *Doctor Who* script books are intended as reference works as well as adaptations. Our aim with the series is to give as true as possible a representation of the programmes as they were broadcast. Accordingly, we shall endeavour to deal with the facts of the programme's history and the creative talents involved in its making.

Each of our books will contain the complete televised script of each story, including the 'cliff-hanger' scenes which regularly ended the final episode of a story and set the scene for the following adventure. Wherever possible, we will talk to the original scriptwriters to discover how their stories were inspired. Of course, since we are dealing with scripts which were written nearly a quarter of a century ago, a number of the authors are now, unfortunately, deceased. This is the case with Anthony Coburn, writer of the first *Doctor Who* story, *The Tribe of Gum*.

As well as scripts, each book will contain the complete cast and production credits for the story plus dates and times of transmission, repeats etc. These should be a rich source of information for completists among the many avid *Doctor Who* fans as well as for serious students of science fiction on television.

While preparing the scripts for publication, we have had to adopt certain conventions in order to make the names of characters consistent. For example, in our version, Ian Chesterton is always called 'Ian'. The scripts for the first story refer to him variously as 'Ian' and 'Chesterton'. Also, we are using the name 'The Doctor', rather than 'Doctor Who' which was frequently used in the early scripts and also appeared in the closing credits at the end of each episode, right up until the late seventies. As it is made quite clear in the second episode of the first story, the 'Who' in 'Doctor Who' was never intended to be a part of his name but rather as an unanswerable question.

For the descriptions of scenes included in this book, we have retained, wherever possible, the descriptions used in the original scripts. Occasionally, when an action occurs on screen which does not reflect what was written in the script we have included our own description of the televised action. An example of this comes near the end of *An Unearthly Child*; in Anthony Coburn's script, it says that the Doctor presses a switch on the TARDIS' console, a warning light flashes and Susan screams a warning to Ian. In the televised version there is no flashing light at this point in the action. This detail, and others like it, have therefore been excluded from the scripts in this book.

Finally we welcome you to send us your views on this and future books in the series. We cannot promise to reply but we will be grateful of the chance to hear your ideas.

John McElroy, October 1987

DOCTOR WHO

THE BEGINNING

Why in 1963 did the BBC transmit a programme about a seven hundred year old man, who travelled through Time and Space in a police box? Was it some kind of joke on the viewers, some brilliant flash of foresight that they were creating a legend, or was it something else?

It was something else.

Doctor Who originally owed its existence to the programme planners of 1963 who wanted to retain the large number of viewers of the afternoon sports programme *Grandstand* through to the pop programme *Juke Box Jury*. At that time the gap was filled by a drama for children, very similar to the *Children's Classic Serial* which is now shown on Sunday afternoons on BBC 1. The planners were still happy with a drama programme in the slot, but wanted one which would hold the sports viewers, grab the attention of those who would watch the pop programme and, on top of all that, be suitable for all the family.

The problem was handed over to the relatively new Head of Drama, Sydney Newman. He was offered various ideas, but none of them appealed to him. However, at the back of his mind, he had the story of H.G. Wells' *The Time Machine*. Gradually, he developed the idea of a man, over seven hundred years old, who was somewhat senile, lost and bewildered, with occasional flashes of extreme brilliance. The old man had come from some distant planet which had been invaded by aliens, and had been trying to return ever since in the time machine in which he had escaped. He did not know exactly how to operate it, because he was senile, and so had become a wanderer in the fourth dimension.

Sydney Newman wanted the time machine to be a commonplace object which, when entered, would be an enormous spaceship. This led to the idea of the camouflage unit (which later became known as the Chameleon Circuit) and the time machine's first appearance as a police telephone box (although it was never explained why there should be a police box in a junk-yard!). As programme planning meetings continued, it soon became obvious that it would cost far too much to build a new time machine exterior for each story, and so it was decided that the ship would become stuck as a police box.

With the basic idea of the new programme settled, Sydney Newman wrote a memorandum to the Head of Serials, Donald Wilson, outlining his ideas. It was received with some reserve, but by no means dismissed.

The next stage was to decide who the Producer would be. The feeling was that there was no one within the BBC who had the sense of levity, wit, humour and yet seriousness inherent in the programme's purpose. It needed someone who would be prepared to break the rules in producing the programme. Then Sydney Newman remembered a production assistant from his time at ATV, Verity Lambert. He contacted Verity and offered her the job of Producer of the new series. After some initial caution, she decided that this would be a great challenge and put all her energy into the new project. This was the first time Verity had produced a programme and so Donald Wilson appointed Mervyn Pinfield as Associate Producer.

The other important member of the production team

was the Script Editor, David Whitaker. He too was caught up in this novel idea of Sydney Newman's and was quickly at work deciding on the cast and their characters. In accordance with the Newman directive, Whitaker included historical stories, alternating them with the science fiction stories: the basic explanation for this being the Doctor's attempts to get Ian and Barbara back to 1963 London. He set the first story in prehistoric times in order to contrast not only with our 'modern' times but also with the advanced technology at the Doctor's disposal.

The next step was to decide who would write the first story, or rather, the first two stories as Whitaker felt that one writer should be used to establish the style of both historical and science fiction stories. He chose the Australian, Anthony Coburn. The first episode, setting the scene of the entire series to follow, had already been outlined by Whitaker and a BBC staff writer C.E. Webber. In consultation with these two, Coburn wrote the final draft of the first episode, changing Susan from just another fugitive from the Doctor's home planet to his granddaughter. A few eyebrows had been raised at the idea of a female teenager travelling with an old man! The last three episodes he provisionally called *The Tribe of Gum*, but it was also known as *100,000 BC*.

It was only at this point that Verity Lambert joined the programme, but there was still a lot to do in getting *Doctor Who*, as the programme had now been titled, on its way to the viewers. (Incidentally, during the early years it was not uncommon to see the programme's title written as *Doctor Who?* and even up to the nineteen-eighties this sometimes appeared.) Obviously, the programme had to grab the viewer's attention as quickly as possible, so Verity Lambert used the BBC's Radiophonic Workshop to create the theme. She hired the versatile and prolific composer Ron Grainer to create the basic part of the theme, which was then 'realised' into electronic sounds by Delia Derbyshire.

The most important decision to be taken next was the choosing of the actor to play the Doctor. Verity Lambert remembered William Hartnell from the ITV series *The Army Game* and the film *This Sporting Life*. Although neither of these show Hartnell acting particularly like the Doctor, Verity Lambert saw the potential for the character of the Doctor in his performance.

With the remaining actors cast, and Warris Hussein chosen to direct the first story, the recording of the pilot episode occurred on 27th September. This was a trial run to see how all the ideas put into the series would come together. The main intention was to judge the characters themselves, and the way their relationships would progress in the future.

The second half of the episode, the TARDIS scene, was recorded twice for this reason. In the first version, Carole Ann Ford played Susan in a very adult and superior manner. Susan was definitely not the child she seemed to be at school. In the second version she was more immature, more like the schoolgirl she was pretending to be.

The Doctor was much more aggressive, contemptuously referring to Ian as 'schoolteacher'. He was not to be bothered by these primitive humans. At the end of the episode it was Ian and the Doctor who fought as the Doctor activated the controls.

The pilot also included technical details which differ from the final version. The theme included a thunderclap/explosion noise just after the title sequence started. The TARDIS hum was very harsh, more like a buzz. The equipment/computer bay behind the scanner contained photo 'blow-ups' of valves and other electronic equipment. These were changed to the simpler, but more futuristic, almost completely blank wall with a few flashing lights on it. The TARDIS dematerialisation noise contained only a few elements of the familiar 'groaning' sound. Most of it seemed to be a variation of 'white noise'.

When the pilot was reviewed, it was quickly obvious that changes would have to be made. If the characters persisted in the manner in which they interacted in the pilot, they would surely be at each other's throats in a very short time. In particular, the Doctor's character needed to be toned down. His aggression was replaced by an aloofness from the situation. Now the humans were of no real importance to him. Susan was obviously identifiable to the audience as a schoolgirl and hence this aspect was given more emphasis.

The script also needed a few alterations. In it, there was a specific mention of the Doctor's and Susan's original time period. It was felt that this immediately dispelled some of the mystery of the series: the less we knew about the Doctor and Susan the better. So it was on 18th October 1963 that *Doctor Who* started recording in earnest. The final version of the first episode was made with almost entirely the same cast, only the policeman being played by a different actor. The TARDIS interior noise was mellowed to a more pleasing hum, and the interior only slightly redesigned. A scene with Susan making an ink-blot pattern on paper in the schoolroom was lost. In the pilot, the Doctor had opened the TARDIS by taking out the police box Yale lock and shining his torch into the hole left behind. In the final version, he simply used a Yale key to open the doors. The TARDIS dematerialisation noise was re-recorded, resulting in the familiar noise still used today.

The sound effect for the TARDIS dematerialisation was produced by running an ordinary Yale key along some piano wires, recording the sound and playing it back at a different speed. Easy, but very effective. In those days, the recording technique was such that the programme had to be recorded almost as if it were live. This was due to the fact that video technology was in its infancy and editing had to be done by hand, physically splicing tapes together. For this reason several scenes were also recorded where one character speaks to another who is heard but not actually seen. This is denoted in the script by *OOV* (Out Of View) next to a character's name. The dialogue of this character would have been pre-recorded and played back so that the character who was in view could respond. This happens most notably in the classroom flashback scenes. In the first episode, there was just one recording break, between the junk-yard scene and the interior of the TARDIS. In Episode Two there was one break after the interior TARDIS scene. Episode Three had two recording breaks, one after the scene where Hur and Za discovered that the TARDIS crew had escaped, and the other after Ian, Susan and Barbara decided to help Za. In Episode Four there were also two breaks, the first after Ian started to make fire, and the second after the crew had run into the Ship (as the TARDIS was often called in those days). This limitation in technology also meant that the sound effects and music had to be incorporated all in one go. The master video recording would play to a sound studio where engineers would be standing by with the sound effects and music on tape. As they watched the episode they would mix in their tapes with the original sound track. If they slightly mistimed a tape then they would just carry on recording. It would only be when they had made a bad mistake, or lots of mistakes, that they would stop and then have to start all over again from the beginning. This often meant that it could take nearly a day to put the sound onto one episode.

The title sequence itself is unique to the nineteen-sixties, and could only be reproduced these days with some considerable difficulty. The technique is quite simple. Point a television camera at a television screen which is showing what the camera sees. This leads to the camera looking at what it's looking at, at what it's looking at, at what it's looking at. . . The images from the screen to the camera, and *vice versa*, build up to an effect known as positive feedback, or 'howl-around'. The patterns are formed by the scanning lines on the television and the fact that the camera is out of alignment. This effect can be reproduced primitively these days with home video cameras. The effect works much better with black and white, and to get the *Doctor Who* effect you would need a camera and television which both work on the obsolete 405 line system (ie 405 lines make up a television picture; these days 625 lines are used in most European countries). Interesting effects can be achieved if a mirror is placed at right angles to the television screen, and the camera directed at the point where the screen and mirror meet. A similar, audio phenomenon occurs when a microphone is placed too near to a loudpeaker that is being used to output the sound from the microphone.

The designer for the pilot was Peter Brachacki. Most of the design requirements were quite standard: schoolroom interiors, Totter's Lane and the junk-yard itself. The school set was cleverly built so that the two classrooms featured were just the two ends of one room. The real challenge for Peter Brachacki was the inside of the Ship. By the time he had finished, the TARDIS set took up almost half the studio.

In consultation with the director and other members of the production team, he envisaged the TARDIS as a solo-operated craft which, accordingly, should have a central control panel with all the controls easily accessible to one person. His original idea for the central column was that it would rise when the TARDIS took off and, when it reached maximum height, would stay there and slowly turn around, while lights inside flashed on and off. Then, when the journey was finished, the column would go down. It was intended to be a type of three-dimensional navigation instrument, which the operator could study and find out where he was in Time and Space. Of course, since the Doctor was not really meant to know quite what was going on in the TARDIS, this idea was never mentioned and the central column was made to go up and down in flight, almost like some strange type of pump propelling the TARDIS through the fourth and fifth dimensions.

The instrumentation on the console was a compromise between Peter Brachacki's wishes and the budget. His intention was to have controls which only fitted the Doctor's hands, emphasising the fact that the Doctor was the only one able to operate the machine. Making special moulds proved too expensive, and so the console was fitted out with a collection of old switches, voltmeters and other odds and ends. Again, the budget put constraints on the original design for the walls. They would have been translucent, made out of fibre glass, and when the TARDIS was in flight would pulsate. In the event, the walls were made from wood with the indents made from fibre glass. Peter Brachacki chose a circular pattern for the walls as he wanted something which would be timeless, something equally suited both to ancient Egypt and the far distant future. One of the walls was simply a giant photographic 'blow-up', taken from an original three-inch-square sheet of plastic!

Originally the TARDIS had two other features, which have long since vanished. The first was a very large object, rather like a giant light, hanging above the set between the doors and the console. This was meant to give the idea of a tremendous power source. The second was a pair of black rectangular boxes which stood against the walls on opposite sides of the console. Again the original idea for these proved impractical. It had been intended that the boxes would be made out of some material which would be capable of changing from opaque to clear, and in flight there would be pulsing lights inside. No material could be found to fulfil this function and so lights inside the semitranslucent boxes simply flashed when the Ship dematerialised.

Although it was Peter Brachacki's intention that the TARDIS interior should give the idea of tremendous power and efficiency, he also added odds and ends of furniture and large *objets d'art*. These were added to emphasise the different time periods which the Doctor had visited and to suggest that he was someone much-travelled.

Unfortunately, Brachacki fell ill before the second recording of the first episode, and his place was taken by Barry Newbery. Few changes were made by him in the first episode. The junk-yard looked slightly different, and the TARDIS computer area behind the scanner was altered. Newbery had to design another side of the TARDIS for the second episode, keeping the now established style of The Ship in mind, and of course he designed all of *The Tribe of Gum* sets.

The pilot and all four episodes were recorded in Studio D at the BBC's Lime Grove studios. Some of the scenes were filmed beforehand at the BBC's studios at Ealing. One of the reasons for this was that the fire regulations at Ealing were less strict than those at Lime Grove, and so all scenes with fire were much easier to film. Another reason was that good fight scenes need a lot of editing, and with the early video technology of the sixties it made sense to do fight scenes on film, particularly the one lasting one minute and forty-five seconds in Episode Four between Kal and Za. Not all the film sequences were filmed with sound. If the scene required no dialogue then it was usually recorded mute and any sound effects, or music, required were added later on.

The music Susan is listening to on the radio in the first episode is really *Three Guitars Mood 2* by the Arthur Nelson Group, and in the same episode nine minutes of Norman Kay's incidental music were used and in the subsequent episodes four minutes, three minutes and ten minutes were used respectively.

There were two promotional trailers for the first episode transmitted by the BBC: one on 16th November 1963 at 5.41 pm and one, six days later, on 22nd November at 5.59 pm. They asked who the mysterious Doctor was and showed a clip of the dematerialisation sequence from the end of the first episode, with the Doctor and then Susan superimposed over it.

For reasons which have long since been forgotten, the first episode was repeated immediately before the second episode at 5.06 pm on 30th November 1963. The most likely reason was the death of President Kennedy on the 22nd November. This caused the BBC to re-schedule its programmes on the 23rd, and so viewers may well have missed the crucial opening episode of the BBC's new series.

Although the production team were very happy with Anthony Coburn's script for the first story, they decided that his science fiction adventure was not what they wanted for the second story, and a script by Terry Nation concerning the planet Skaro was used instead. Sadly therefore, Anthony Coburn's superb *The Masters of Luxor* was never to reach our television screens. . .

MAIN CAST:

The Doctor .... William Hartnell
Ian Chesterton .... William Russell
Barbara Wright .... Jacqueline Hill
Susan Foreman .... Carole Ann Ford
Policeman .... Reg Cranfield
Kal .... Jeremy Young
Za .... Derek Newark
Hur .... Alethea Charlton
Old Mother .... Eileen Way
Horg .... Howard Lang

SUPPORTING CAST:

Schoolchildren .... Carole Clarke
Mavis Ranson
Francesco Bertorelli
Heather Lyons
Cedric Schoeman
Richard Wilson
Brian Thomas

Shadow of Za .... Leslie Bates

Tribesmen .... Frank Wheatley
Al Davis
Roy Denton
Bill Nicholas
Billie Davis
Leslie Bates
Bob Haddow

Tribeswomen .... Jean Denyer
Margot Maxine (Episode 2)
Brenda Proctor
Elizabeth Body
Veronica Dyson
Diane Gay
Doreen Ubells
Lyn Turner

Tribeschildren .... Antonia Moss (Episode 2)
David Rosen (Episodes 2,3,4)
Julie Moss (Episode 2)
Trevor Thomas (Episode 2)
Elizabeth White (Episodes 3,4)
Janet Fairhead (Episodes 3, 4)
Timothy Palmer (Episodes 3,4)

Stand-Ins .... Derek Ware*
Billy Cornelius*

plus 12 extras (on film only)

* Stunt-men used for fight sequence in Episode 4

Story Code: A*

Story Title(s): An Unearthly Child**
                 The Tribe of Gum
                 100,000 Years BC

Episode One

Title .... An Unearthly Child
Duration .... 23'23"
Author .... Anthony Coburn/C.E. Webber
Pilot Recorded .... 27th September 1963
Re-recorded .... 18th October 1963
First Transmitted ..... 23rd November 1963, at 17:16:20
Repeated .... 30th November 1963, at 17:06:19
                        2nd November 1981, at 17:39:35†

* The stories were coded alphabetically for easy reference.

** It is thought likely that the title *An Unearthly Child* was only ever
intended to refer to the first episode, and that the other two titles were
only intended to cover Episodes 2 – 4. Indeed, were it not for the story

Episode Two

Title .... The Cave of Skulls
Duration .... 24'36"
Author .... Anthony Coburn
Recorded .... 25th October 1963
First Transmitted ..... 30th November 1963, at 17:29:52
Repeated .... 3rd November 1981, at 17:39:03

Episode Three

Title .... The Forest of Fear
Duration .... 23'38"
Author .... Anthony Coburn
Recorded .... 1st November 1963
First Transmitted ..... 7th December 1963, at 17:15:30
Repeated .... 4th November 1981, at 17:40:22

Episode Four

Title .... The Firemaker
Duration .... 24'22"
Author .... Anthony Coburn
Recorded .... 8th November 1963
First Transmitted ..... 14th December 1963, at 17:14:58
Repeated .... 5th November 1981, at 17:41:19

code, it would be reasonable to think of these episodes as a one-part story plus a three-parter. However, since all four episodes have the same story code, *The Tribe of Gum* is usually used when referring to all of them as one story. Curiously, there is no record of the actual name 'Gum' occurring in any of the scripts.

† Repeated as the first of *The Five Faces of Doctor Who* on BBC 2.

PRODUCTION CREDITS

Producer .... Verity Lambert
Associate Producer .... Mervyn Pinfield
Script Editor .... David Whitaker
Director .... Warris Hussein
Designer .... Peter Brachacki (Pilot)
Barry Newbery
(Episodes 1 – 4) *

Technical Operations Manager
.... Ken MacGregor
Lighting Supervisor .... S. Barclay (Pilot)
Geoff Shaw
Sound Supervisor .... Jack Clayton
Vision Mixer .... Clive Doig
Grams. Operator .... Adrian Bishop-Laggett
Production Assistant .... Douglas Camfield
(Episodes 1,2,4)
Production Assistant .... Tony Lightley
(Episode 3)
Assistant Floor Manager .... Catherine Childs
Floor Assistant .... Robert Fort
Assistant .... Peggy Lupton

* Although Peter Brachacki is credited as designer at the end of Episode
One, in fact Barry Newbery 're-set' it.

Secretary .... Margaret Allen
Costume Supervisor .... Maureen Heneghan
Make-up Supervisor .... Betty Blattner
Title music composed by .... Ron Grainer
Title music realised by .... Delia Derbyshire
Incidental music .... Norman Kay
Special Effects .... BBC Visual Effects
                                      Department
Camera Crew .... Number One Crew

AN UNEARTHLY CHILD

1. A STREET (NIGHT).

(The time is three o'clock in the morning. It is dark and foggy. In the street we hear the striking of a nearby clock. A policeman approaches holding out his torch to see where he is going. He stops and turns round to examine the written notice on a pair of large gates: 'I.M. FOREMAN – Scrap Merchants, Totter's Lane'. The policeman pushes the gates and as he walks away they swing open. The camera slowly pans round the junk-yard, finally coming to rest on a police box, from which comes an eerie humming sound, suggesting hidden power.)

2. A CORRIDOR IN A SCHOOL (LATE AFTERNOON).

(A small number of children, all about fourteen or fifteen years old, enter the corridor from a classroom. They are

obviously going home. An older woman also leaves the classroom, their teacher, BARBARA WRIGHT. *As she leaves, she turns back and speaks to someone still in the classroom.)*

BARBARA: Wait in here please, Susan. I won't be long.

*(*BARBARA *walks down the corridor, and enters another room.)*

3. SCIENCE LABORATORY.

*(*IAN CHESTERTON, *a science teacher is sitting on a stool writing in a folder.)*

IAN: Not gone yet?

BARBARA: Obviously not.

IAN: Ask a silly question.

BARBARA: I'm sorry.

IAN: It's all right. I forgive you this time.

BARBARA: Oh, I've had a terrible day. I don't know what to make of it.

IAN: What's the trouble. Can I help?

BARBARA: Oh, it's one of the girls. Susan Foreman.

IAN: Susan Foreman! Oh, she your problem too?

BARBARA (*oov*): Yes.

IAN: And you don't know what to make of her?

BARBARA (*oov*): No.

IAN: How old is she, Barbara?

BARBARA: Fifteen.

IAN: Fifteen. . . She lets her knowledge out a bit at a time so as not to embarrass me. That's what I feel about her. She knows more Science than I'll ever know. She's a genius. Is that what she's doing with History?

BARBARA: Something like that.

IAN: So your problem is whether to stay in business or hand over the class to her?

BARBARA: No, not quite.

   (IAN _laughs._)

IAN: What then?

BARBARA: Ian, I must talk to someone about this, but I don't want to get the girl into trouble. And I know you're going to tell me I'm imagining things.

IAN: No, I'm not.

BARBARA: Well, I told you how good she is at History. I had a talk with her and I told her she ought to specialise. . . Well, she seemed quite interested 'til I said I'd be willing to work with her at her home. Then she said that would be absolutely impossible as her grandfather didn't like strangers.

IAN: He's a doctor, isn't he? That's a bit of a lame excuse.

BARBARA: Well, I didn't pursue the point, but then recently her homework's been so bad.

> (IAN *gets up and starts to wash his hands.*)

IAN: Yes, I know.

BARBARA: Finally, I was so irritated with all her excuses, I decided to have a talk with this grandfather of hers and tell him to take some interest in her.

IAN: Oh, did you indeed? And what's the old boy like?

BARBARA: That's just it. I got her address from the secretary: 76 Totter's Lane, and I went along there one evening. Oh Ian, do pay attention!

IAN: Sorry. You went along there one evening?

BARBARA: Well, there isn't anything there. It's just an old junk-yard.

IAN: You must have gone to the wrong place.

BARBARA: Well, that was the address the secretary gave me.

IAN: Well, the secretary got it wrong then.

BARBARA: No! I checked. There's a big wall on one side, houses on the other, and nothing in the middle. And this nothing in the middle is number 76 Totter's Lane.

IAN: Hm. That's a bit of a mystery. Well, there must be a simple answer somewhere.

BARBARA: Well what?

IAN: Well, we'll have to find out for ourselves, won't we?

BARBARA: Thank you for the 'we'. She's waiting in one of the classrooms, I'm lending her a book on the French Revolution.

IAN: What's she going to do – re-write it? All right. What do we do, ask her point-blank?

BARBARA: No, I thought we could drive there, wait 'til she arrives and see where she goes.

IAN: Oh, all right.

BARBARA: Well, that is if you're not doing anything.

IAN: No, I'm not. After you.

(They leave the room.)

4. CLASSROOM.

(SUSAN is listening to a small transistor radio which she holds to her ear. She is swaying to the music, gesturing strangely with her right hand, oblivious to the fact that BARBARA and IAN have entered.)

BARBARA: Susan. . . .

SUSAN: Oh, I'm sorry Miss Wright, didn't hear you coming in. Aren't they fabulous?

BARBARA: Who?

SUSAN: It's John Smith and the Common Men. They've gone from nineteen to two.

BARBARA: Eh?

IAN: John Smith is the stage name of the Honourable Aubrey Waites. He started his career as Chris Waites and the Carollers, didn't he Susan?

SUSAN: You are surprising, Mr. Chesterton. I wouldn't expect you to know things like that.

IAN: Oh, I have an enquiring mind. And a very sensitive ear.

SUSAN: Oh. I'm sorry.

(She turns off the radio.)

IAN: Thank you.

SUSAN: Is that the book you promised me?

BARBARA: Yes.

SUSAN: Thank you very much. It will be interesting. I'll return it tomorrow.

BARBARA: Oh, that's not necessary. Keep it until you've finished it.

SUSAN: I'll have finished it.

IAN: Where do you live, Susan? I'm giving Miss Wright a lift. I've room for one more.

SUSAN: No thank you, Mr. Chesterton. I like walking through the dark. It's mysterious.

BARBARA: Be careful, Susan. There'll probably be fog again tonight. See you in the morning.

SUSAN: I expect so. Good night.

BARBARA: Good night.

IAN: Good night, Susan.

> (IAN *and* BARBARA *leave the classroom. As soon as they have gone,* SUSAN *opens the book and starts to read. She frowns, and mutters to herself in indignation.*)

SUSAN: That's not right.

5. CORNER OF TOTTER'S LANE (NIGHT).

> (IAN *and* BARBARA *are in a car,* IAN *is driving. He puts on the handbrake, switches off the engine and the lights.*)

BARBARA: Over there.

IAN: Lucky there was no fog. I'd never have found this.

BARBARA: Well, she doesn't seem to have arrived yet. I suppose we are doing the right thing, aren't we?

> (*She looks at* IAN.)

IAN: You can't justify curiosity.

BARBARA: But her homework. . . ?

IAN: Bit of an excuse, really, isn't it? I've seen far worse. The truth is we're both curious about Susan, and we won't be happy until we know some of the answers.

BARBARA: You can't just pass it off like that. If I thought I was just being a busybody I'd go straight home. I thought you agreed she was a bit of a mystery.

IAN: Yes. . . but I think you'll find there's a very simple explanation to all this.

BARBARA: Well, I don't know how you explain the fact that a teenage girl does not know how many shillings there are in a pound.

IAN: Really?

BARBARA: Really. She said she thought we were on the decimal system.

IAN: Decimal system?

6. CLASSROOM (DAY).

(There is laughter in the classroom. SUSAN *is sitting at her desk, very embarrassed, having realised that she has just made a mistake.)*

SUSAN: I'm sorry, Miss Wright.

BARBARA: Don't be silly, Susan. The United States has a decimal system, you know perfectly well that we do not.

SUSAN: Of course, the decimal system hasn't started yet.

7. INSIDE THE CAR (NIGHT).

IAN: I suppose she couldn't be a foreigner. No, it doesn't make sense. Nothing about this girl makes sense! For instance, the other day I was talking about chemical changes. I'd given out the litmus paper to show cause and effect.

BARBARA: And she knew the answer before you'd started.

IAN: Well, not quite. The answer simply didn't interest her.

8. SCIENCE LABORATORY (DAY).

SUSAN: Yes, I can see red turns to blue, Mr. Chesterton, but that's because we're dealing with two inactive chemicals. They only act in relation to each other.

IAN (*OOV*):   But that's the whole point of the experiment, Susan.

SUSAN: Yes, it's a bit obvious, isn't it? Well, I'm not trying to be rude but couldn't we deal with two active chemicals? Then red could turn blue all by itself and we could get on with something else. I'm sorry, it was just an idea.

   (*She subsides, conscious that again she has said too much.*)

9. INSIDE THE CAR (NIGHT).

IAN: She means it. These simple experiments are child's play to her.

BARBARA: It's almost got to the point where I deliberately want to trip her up.

IAN: Yes . . . something like that happened the other day. I'd set the class a problem with A, B and C as the three dimensions.

10. CLASSROOM (DAY).

(Susan is at the blackboard, visibly upset.)

SUSAN: It's impossible unless you use D and E.

IAN (*oov*): D and E. Whatever for? Do the problem that's set, Susan.

SUSAN: I can't, Mr. Chesterton. You can't simply work on three of the dimensions.

IAN (*oov*): Three of them? Oh, Time being the fourth, I suppose? What do you need E for? What do you make the fifth dimension?

SUSAN: Space.

11. INSIDE THE CAR (NIGHT).

BARBARA: Too many questions and not enough answers.

IAN: Stupid? Or just doesn't know? So we have a fifteen year old girl, who is absolutely brilliant at some things and excruciatingly bad at others.

BARBARA: There she is.

(SUSAN _approaches, looks around, opens the gates and goes in, closing them again behind her._)

BARBARA: Look, can we go in? I hate to think of her alone in that place.

IAN: If she is alone. Look, she is fifteen. She might be meeting a boy. Didn't that occur to you?

BARBARA: Well, I almost hope she is.

IAN: What do you mean?

BARBARA: Well, it would be so wonderfully normal. Silly, isn't it? I feel frightened. As if we were about to interfere in something that is best left alone.

12. INSIDE THE JUNK-YARD.

(SUSAN _pops a sweet into her mouth. She moves off._)

13. INSIDE THE CAR.

IAN: Come on. Let's get it over with.

(They both get out of the car and cross over to enter the yard.)

BARBARA: Well, don't you feel it?

IAN: I take things as they come. Come on.

14. *INSIDE THE JUNK-YARD.*

IAN: What a mess. I'm not turning over any of this stuff to find her.

BARBARA: Over there?

(IAN trips over.)

IAN: Blast! I've dropped it.

BARBARA: What?

IAN: The torch.

BARBARA: Well, use a match.

IAN: I haven't got any. Oh never mind.

BARBARA: Susan?

(Silence.)

IAN: Susan. . . Susan. . .

(IAN climbs up some steps and then down again.)

IAN: Susan. . . Susan. . . Mr. Chesterton and Miss Wright.

(Silence.)

IAN: She can't have got out without us seeing her.

BARBARA: Ian, look at this.

IAN: Well, it's a police box. What on earth's it doing here? These things are usually on the street. . .

(As he is saying this, he goes up to the box, and touches it.)

IAN: Feel it. Feel it. You feel it?

(BARBARA does so.)

BARBARA: It's a faint vibration.

IAN: It's alive!

(IAN walks around the police box.)

IAN: It's not connected to anything. Unless it's through the floor.

BARBARA: Look, I've had enough. Let's go and find a policeman.

IAN: Yes, all right.

(We hear the sound of coughing.)

BARBARA: Is that her?

IAN: That's not her. Quick!

> *(He pulls her down behind a pile of junk in a corner. We now catch our first glimpse of* THE DOCTOR *as he enters the yard. He is wearing a long, dark cloak, with a scarf wrapped around his shoulders, and a hat. His clothes are somewhat unusual. He stands, coughing, for a moment. He moves across the yard, and approaches the police box.* THE DOCTOR *takes out an ordinary door key, and inserts it in the lock.* SUSAN'*s voice can be heard.)*

SUSAN (*oov*): There you are, Grandfather.

BARBARA: It's Susan!

IAN: Ssh!

> *(*THE DOCTOR *hears this and turns towards where* IAN *and* BARBARA *are hiding.* IAN *stands up and moves towards* THE DOCTOR.*)*

IAN: Excuse me. . .

THE DOCTOR: What are you doing here?

IAN: We're looking for a girl.

THE DOCTOR: We?

> *(*BARBARA *comes out of the shadows.)*

BARBARA: Good evening.

> *(*THE DOCTOR *regards her carefully.)*

THE DOCTOR: What do you want?

IAN: One of our pupils, Susan Foreman, came into this yard.

THE DOCTOR: Really? In here? Are you sure?

BARBARA: Yes, we saw her from across the street.

(THE DOCTOR *mutters to himself.*)

THE DOCTOR: One of their pupils . . . not the police then.

IAN: I beg your pardon?

THE DOCTOR: Why were you spying on her? Who are you?

IAN: We heard a young girl's voice call out to you.

THE DOCTOR: Your hearing must be very acute. I didn't hear anything.

BARBARA: It came from in here.

THE DOCTOR: You imagined it.

BARBARA: I certainly did not imagine it.

(THE DOCTOR *takes* IAN *by the arm and leads him away from the police box.*)

THE DOCTOR: Young man, is it reasonable to suppose that anybody would be inside a cupboard like that? Hmm?

IAN: Would it therefore be unreasonable to ask you to let us have a look inside?

(THE DOCTOR *notices a picture frame.*)

THE DOCTOR: I wonder why I've never seen that before.

Now isn't that strange . . . very damp . . . and dirty.

BARBARA: Won't you help us? We're two of her teachers from the Coal Hill School. We saw her come in and we haven't seen her leave. Naturally, we're worried.

THE DOCTOR: It'll have to be cleaned. Hm. Oh, I'm afraid it's none of my business. I suggest you leave here.

(He puts the picture frame down.)

IAN: Not until we're satisfied that Susan isn't here. And, frankly, I don't understand your attitude.

THE DOCTOR: Yours leaves a lot to be desired.

IAN: Will you open the door?

THE DOCTOR: There's nothing in there.

IAN: Then what are you afraid to show us?

THE DOCTOR: Afraid? Oh, go away!

IAN: I think we'd better go and fetch a policeman.

THE DOCTOR: Very well.

IAN: And you're coming with us.

THE DOCTOR: Oh, am I?

(He laughs.)

THE DOCTOR: I don't think so, young man. No, I don't think so.

BARBARA: We can't force him.

IAN: But we can't leave him here. Doesn't it seem obvious to you that he's got her locked up in there? Look at it. There's no door-handle. Must be a secret lock somewhere.

> (THE DOCTOR *examines a small jug, listening carefully to their conversation.*)

BARBARA: That was Susan's voice. . .

IAN: Of course it was. Susan. . . Susan. . . Are you in there? It's Mr. Chesterton and Miss Wright, Susan.

THE DOCTOR: Don't you think you're being rather high-handed, young man? You thought you saw a young girl enter the yard. You imagine you heard her voice. You believe she might be in there. It's not very substantial, is it?

> (*He puts the jug down.*)

BARBARA: But why won't you help us?

THE DOCTOR: I'm not hindering you. If you both want to make fools of yourselves, I suggest you do what you said you'd do. Go and find a policeman.

IAN: While you nip off quietly in the other direction.

THE DOCTOR: Insulting! There's only one way in and out of this yard. I shall be here when you get back.

I want to see your faces when you try to explain away your behaviour to a policeman.

IAN: Nevertheless, we're going to find one. Come on, Barbara.

(They start to leave. Just then, they hear SUSAN*'s voice again.)*

SUSAN (*oov*): What are you doing out there?

IAN: She *is* in there!

THE DOCTOR: Close the door.

*(*IAN *grabs* THE DOCTOR*'s arm.)*

IAN: Barbara!

*(*BARBARA *rushes through the door.)*

15. INSIDE THE SHIP.

*(*BARBARA *and then* IAN *enter.* SUSAN *is standing there by a hexagonal control console in the centre of the room. She stares at them in amazement.* IAN *stops and looks around.* THE DOCTOR *enters behind them.)*

THE DOCTOR: Close the doors, Susan.

*(*SUSAN *flicks a switch on the console, and the doors close.)*

THE DOCTOR: I believe these people are known to you?

(SUSAN *addresses* THE DOCTOR *and then*
IAN *and* BARBARA.)

SUSAN: They're two of my schoolteachers. What are
you doing here?

BARBARA: Where are we?

THE DOCTOR: They must have followed you. That ridiculous school! I knew something like this
would happen if we stayed in one place too
long.

SUSAN: Why should they follow me?

BARBARA: Is this really where you live, Susan?

SUSAN: Yes.

THE DOCTOR: And what's wrong with it?

IAN: But it was just a telephone box!

THE DOCTOR: Perhaps.

BARBARA: And this is your grandfather?

SUSAN: Yes.

BARBARA: Well, why didn't you tell us that?

THE DOCTOR: I don't discuss my private life with strangers.

IAN: But it was a police telephone box. I walked
all round it. Barbara, you saw me.

THE DOCTOR: You don't deserve any explanations. You
pushed your way in here, uninvited and
unwelcome.

BARBARA: I think we ought to leave.

IAN: Just a minute. I know this is absurd, but. . .

> (THE DOCTOR *studies a clock on a pedestal.)*

THE DOCTOR: Dear, dear, dear, dear. This is very unreliable. . .

IAN: I walked all around it. . .

THE DOCTOR: It's stopped again, you know, and I've tried. . . Hm? Oh, you wouldn't understand.

IAN: But I want to understand.

THE DOCTOR: Yes, yes, yes, yes, yes, yes. Oh! By the way, Susan, I managed to find a replacement for that faulty filament. Bit of an amateur job, but I think it'll serve.

IAN: It's an illusion, it must be.

THE DOCTOR: What is he talking about now?

SUSAN: What are you doing here?

THE DOCTOR: You don't understand, so you find excuses. Illusions indeed! You say you can't fit an enormous building into one of your smaller sitting rooms.

IAN: No. . .

THE DOCTOR: But you've discovered television, haven't you?

IAN: Yes.

THE DOCTOR: Then by showing an enormous building on your television screen, you can do what seemed impossible, couldn't you?

IAN: Well yes, but I still don't. . .

THE DOCTOR: No. Not quite clear is it? I can see by your face that you're not certain. You don't understand.

(He laughs.)

THE DOCTOR: And I knew you wouldn't. Never mind. Now then, which switch was it? No, no, no. Ah yes, that is it. . . The point is not whether you understand . . . what is going to happen to you? Hm? They'll tell everybody about the Ship now.

IAN: 'Ship'?

THE DOCTOR: Yes, yes, Ship. This doesn't roll along on wheels, you know.

BARBARA: You mean . . . it moves?

SUSAN: The TARDIS can go anywhere.

BARBARA: 'Tardis'? I don't understand you, Susan.

SUSAN: Well, I made up the name 'TARDIS' from the initials. Time And Relative Dimension In Space. I thought you'd both understand when you saw the different dimensions inside from those outside.

IAN: Let me get this straight. A thing that looks like a police box standing in a junk-yard. It can move anywhere – in Time and Space.

SUSAN: Yes.

THE DOCTOR: Quite so.

IAN: But that's ridiculous.

SUSAN: Why won't they believe us?

BARBARA: Well, how can we?

THE DOCTOR: Now, now, don't get exasperated, Susan. Remember the Red Indian. When he saw the first steam train, his savage mind thought it an illusion too.

IAN: You're treating us like children.

THE DOCTOR: Am I? The children of my civilisation would be insulted.

IAN: Your civilisation. . . ?

THE DOCTOR: Yes, my civilisation. I tolerate this century, but I don't enjoy it. Have you ever thought what it is like to be wanderers in the fourth dimension, have you? To be exiles . . . Susan and I are cut off from our own planet, without friends or protection. But one day . . . we shall get back. Yes, one day . . . one day.

(IAN and BARBARA look at SUSAN in sheer disbelief.)

SUSAN: It's true. Every word of it's true. You don't know what you've done, coming here.

(She turns desperately to THE DOCTOR.)

SUSAN: Grandfather, let them go now, please. Look if they don't understand they can't . . . they can't hurt us at all. I understand these people better than you. Their minds reject things they don't understand.

THE DOCTOR: No.

IAN: He can't keep us here.

BARBARA: Susan, listen to me. Can't you see that all this is an illusion. It's a game that you and your grandfather are playing, if you like, but you can't expect us to believe it.

SUSAN: It's *not* a game.

BARBARA: But Susan!

SUSAN: It's not! Look, I love your school. I love England in the twentieth century. The last five months have been the happiest of my life.

BARBARA: But you are one of us. You look like us. You sound like us.

SUSAN: I was born in another time, another world.

IAN: Now look here, Susan, you. . . Oh come on Barbara, let's get out of here.

(They move towards the doors.)

SUSAN: No, you two can't get out, he won't let you go.

(They try unsuccessfully to open the doors. IAN *turns angrily to* THE DOCTOR, *who is laughing.)*

IAN: You closed the doors from over there. I saw you. Which is it? Which is it? Which control operates the doors?

*(*IAN *approaches the control console, and realises just how complicated it is.)*

THE DOCTOR: You still think it's all an illusion?

IAN: I know that free movement in Time and Space is a scientific dream I don't expect to find solved in a junk-yard.

THE DOCTOR: Your arrogance is nearly as great as your ignorance!

IAN: Will you open the door? Open the door! Susan, will you help us?

SUSAN: I mustn't.

IAN: Very well then. I'll have to risk it myself.

THE DOCTOR: I can't stop you.

> (THE DOCTOR *quietly operates a switch on the console.* SUSAN *realises too late what* THE DOCTOR *has done, and screams a warning to* IAN.)

SUSAN: Oh, don't touch it! It's live.

> (IAN's *hand reaches the control. There is a crackle, and* IAN *is violently thrown to the floor.* THE DOCTOR *looks on in triumph.* BARBARA *rushes to* IAN, *who is shaken but otherwise unhurt.*)

BARBARA: Ian!

> (*She turns angrily on* THE DOCTOR.)

BARBARA: What on earth do you think you're doing?

SUSAN: Grandfather, let them go now, please.

THE DOCTOR: And by tomorrow we shall be a public spect-
acle, a subject for news and idle gossip.

SUSAN: But they won't say anything.

THE DOCTOR: My dear child, of course they will. Put
yourself in their place. They're bound to
make some sort of a complaint to the
authorities, or at the very least talk to
their friends. If I do let them go, Susan,
you realise of course we must go too?

SUSAN: No. Grandfather, we've had all this out.

THE DOCTOR: There's no alternative, child.

SUSAN: I want to stay. Look, they're both kind
people. Why don't you trust them? All
you've got to do is ask them to promise to
keep our secret and. . .

THE DOCTOR: It's out of the question.

SUSAN: I won't go, Grandfather. I won't leave the
Twentieth Century. I'd . . . I'd rather
leave the TARDIS and you.

THE DOCTOR: Now you're being sentimental and childish.

SUSAN: No, I mean it.

THE DOCTOR: Very well. Then you must go with them. I'll
open the doors.

(THE DOCTOR *walks over to the console.*)

BARBARA: Are you coming, Susan?

(*As* SUSAN *is distracted by* BARBARA'S

question, THE DOCTOR *starts operating the controls on the console. Too late,* SUSAN *realises what he is doing.)*

SUSAN: Oh no, Grandfather, no!

*(*SUSAN *tries to pull* THE DOCTOR *away from the controls.)*

THE DOCTOR: Let me go! Get back to the Ship's side. . . Hold it.

(The lights grow brighter and then darker, and the central column starts to rise. THE DOCTOR *breaks free and operates some further controls.* IAN *and* BARBARA *are tossed helplessly around. On the scanner we see a picture of London rapidly fading into the distance, as if the Ship has taken off like a rocket. This merges into the title sequence effect, superimposed over which we see first the face of* THE DOCTOR *and then that of* SUSAN.

The pattern resolves into a barren landscape. Inside the Ship, THE DOCTOR *and* SUSAN *stand, rather shocked.* BARBARA *has collapsed into a chair and* IAN *is unconscious on the floor. Outside the Ship, a human-like shadow falls across the landscape. . .)*

Next Episode:
THE CAVE OF SKULLS

EPISODE TWO

THE CAVE OF SKULLS

1. The Tribe Encampment (Day).

(The tribespeople are watching ZA *as he squats in front of the dead fire. The atmosphere is tense with expectation and* ZA*'s face registers concentration and desperation as he rubs his hands fiercely together. He is watched by the girl,* HUR, *who holds a folded skin containing the ashes from a fire, long dead. Other members of the tribe, old men, women, and a handful of children, watch, spellbound by* ZA*'s gestures. He rubs a bone between his hands over the woodpile and sprinkles ashes on it. We move away from the crowd, to see the* OLD MOTHER *sitting by herself.)*

OLD MOTHER: Where is the fire Za makes?

HUR: In his hands. It will not go into the wood.

ZA: My father made fire.

OLD MOTHER: They killed him for it. It is better that we live as we have always done.

ZA: He showed me how to sharpen the stones, and trap the bear and the tiger. He should have shown me this too.

OLD MOTHER: So that everyone would bow to you as they did to him?

(ZA *rubs the bone more quickly and leaps over to the* OLD MOTHER.)

ZA: Tell me what my father did to make fire.

OLD MOTHER: I never saw him make it. That is all I know.

ZA: Aaaah! Out of my sight, old woman. You should have died with him.

OLD MOTHER: Za will never make fire.

(ZA *looks despondently at the pile of sticks. He yells in frustration.*)

ZA: Put on more of the dead fire.

(*As* HUR *does so, he begins again to fiercely rub the bone between his hands.*)

HUR: The old men are talking against you, Za. They say it would be better for the stranger, Kal, to lead us.

ZA: Kal!

HUR: They say you sit all day rubbing your hands together while he brings us meat.

ZA: Without meat, we go hungry. Without fire, we die.

HUR: Old men see no further than tomorrow's meat. They will make Kal the leader. My father will give me to him.

ZA: Kal is no leader!

HUR: The leader is the one who makes fire.

(ZA rubs the bone harder still and then raises his arms. Both of them look hopefully at the pile. Nothing happens. ZA sweeps the pile away with a blow from his fist.)

ZA: Where has the fire gone? Where? Where?!!

2. INSIDE THE TARDIS.

(The camera pulls back from a close-up of BARBARA, slumped in a chair. She recovers consciousness and tries to wake IAN who is still slumped on the floor.)

BARBARA: Ian. . . Ian. . .

IAN: I'm all right. . .

(He sits up, holding his head.)

IAN: Oh! I must have hit my head. . . The movement's stopped.

(There is the sound of the Ship's humming. THE DOCTOR *and* SUSAN *stand at the controls, staring at the scanner screen.)*

SUSAN: The base is steady.

*(*THE DOCTOR *is looking up at the scanner.)*

THE DOCTOR: Layer of sand . . . rock formation. . . Mm. Good.

*(*SUSAN *turns now and looks sadly at* BARBARA *and* IAN.*)*

SUSAN: We've left 1963.

THE DOCTOR: Oh yes, undoubtedly. I'll be able to tell you where presently.

(He looks enquiringly at a dial on the console.)

THE DOCTOR: Zero? That's not right. I'm afraid this yearometer is not calculating properly. Humph! Well, anyway, the journey's finished.

(He suddenly notices IAN *and* BARBARA.*)*

THE DOCTOR: What are you doing down there?

BARBARA: What have you done?

IAN: Barbara! You don't believe all this
                nonsense!

SUSAN: Well, look at the scanner screen.

THE DOCTOR: Yes, look up there. They don't understand
                and I suspect they don't want to.

                (He gestures at the scanner. IAN *and*
                BARBARA *get up and stand between
                him and* SUSAN.*)*

THE DOCTOR: Well, there you are. A new world for you.

                *(*IAN *and* BARBARA *look at the scanner
                screen.)*

IAN: Sand and rock?

THE DOCTOR: Yes, that's the immediate view outside the
                Ship.

BARBARA: But where are we?

IAN: You mean that's what we'll see when we go
                outside?

SUSAN: Yes, you'll see it for yourself.

IAN: I don't believe it.

THE DOCTOR: You really are a stubborn young man, aren't
                you?

IAN: All right. Show me some proof. Give me
                some concrete evidence.

                (He turns to SUSAN.*)*

IAN: I'm sorry Susan, I don't want to hurt you, but . . . it's time you were brought back to reality.

SUSAN: But you're wrong, Mr. Chesterton.

THE DOCTOR: They're saying I'm a charlatan. What concrete evidence would satisfy you? Hm?

IAN: Just open the doors, Doctor Foreman.

(THE DOCTOR mutters to himself.)

THE DOCTOR: Eh? Doctor who? What's he talking about?

BARBARA: They're so sure, Ian. . .

IAN: Yes I know, but. . .

BARBARA: And remember the difference between the outside of the police box and the inside.

IAN: Yes I know, but are you going to open the doors, or aren't you?

THE DOCTOR: No.

(IAN turns to BARBARA.)

IAN: You see?

THE DOCTOR: Not until I'm quite sure it's safe to do so.

(He studies the dials.)

THE DOCTOR: Well, the air's good. Yes, it is. It's good. Excellent. Excellent. Have you got the radiation counter there? What does it read?

SUSAN: It's reading normal, Grandfather.

THE DOCTOR: Splendid. Splendid. Well I think I'll take my Geiger counter with me, in any case.

(He turns his attention back to IAN.*)*

THE DOCTOR: So you still challenge me, young man?

IAN: Well, just open the doors and prove your point.

THE DOCTOR: You're so narrow-minded, aren't you? Don't be so insular.

SUSAN: Grandfather. Do you know where we are?

THE DOCTOR: Yes, we've gone back in time all right. One or two samples and I shall be able to make an estimate. Rock pieces and a few plants. But I do wish this wouldn't keep letting me down. However, we can go out now.

IAN: Just a minute. You say we've gone back in time?

THE DOCTOR: Yes. Quite so.

IAN: So that when we go out of that door, we won't be in a junk-yard in London, in England, in the year 1963?

THE DOCTOR: That is quite correct. But your tone suggests ridicule.

IAN: But it is ridiculous. Time doesn't go round and round in circles. You can't get on and off whenever you like in the past or the future.

THE DOCTOR: Really? Where does Time go then?

IAN (*oov*): It doesn't go anywhere. It just happens and then it's finished.

(THE DOCTOR laughs and looks at BARBARA.)

THE DOCTOR: You're not as doubtful as your friend, I hope?

BARBARA: No.

IAN: Barbara! You can't. . .

BARBARA: I can't help it. . . I just believe them, that's all.

THE DOCTOR: If you could touch the alien sand and hear the cries of strange birds, and watch them wheel in another sky – would that satisfy you?

IAN: Yes.

(THE DOCTOR smiles. He turns and pulls a switch. The doors start to open. Through them we see the strange landscape.)

THE DOCTOR: Now, see for yourself.

IAN: It's not true. It can't be.

SUSAN: That's not on the screen.

THE DOCTOR: Well, I've no more time to argue with you. I must get some samples, Susan.

(He picks up a bag, his hat and a Geiger counter and strides out, muttering to himself.)

SUSAN: Be careful, Grandfather.

(BARBARA *goes out slowly after* THE DOCTOR. *We see her stop outside the door and look around.*)

BARBARA: Ian, come out and look.

(IAN *goes to move, but he aches in every limb and winces with pain.* SUSAN *goes to help him.*)

SUSAN: Lean on me.

IAN: Thank you. I'm all right. Thanks.

(*As they leave the Ship, the doors close behind them.*)

3. *ROCKY ENCLOSURE.*

(*In the background is the police box.* IAN *and* SUSAN *step away from it as the doors close.*)

SUSAN: Well?

IAN: But . . . there must be some explanation.

(THE DOCTOR *is now some distance from them. He is again muttering to himself.*)

THE DOCTOR: It's still a police box. Why hasn't it changed? Dear, dear. How very disturbing.

(THE DOCTOR leaves the others. He bends down to examine a piece of rock. Behind THE DOCTOR, we see the face of the watching KAL.)

4. SAND DUNES.

(Meanwhile, we return to the others outside the TARDIS. Part of a large skull sticks out from the sand. BARBARA kneels down by the bone, and is soon joined by SUSAN.)

BARBARA: What do you think it could be? . . . Ian, look at this.

(IAN crouches down beside them.)

IAN: I don't know. Hasn't got any horns or antlers. Could be a horse . . . could be anything.

(He gets up and looks around, and speaks in a whisper to himself.)

IAN: Incredible . . . police box in the midst of . . . it just doesn't make sense. . .

(SUSAN looks up.)

SUSAN: It should have changed. . . I wonder why it hasn't happened this time?

BARBARA: The Ship, you mean?

SUSAN: Yes, it's been an Ionic column and a sedan chair. . .

BARBARA: Disguising itself wherever it goes.

SUSAN: Yes, that's right. But it hasn't happened this time. I wonder why not? Wonder if this old head would help Grandfather? Where is he?

(She stands up to look around, and goes off to look for THE DOCTOR.*)*

BARBARA: You're very quiet.

IAN: I was wrong, wasn't I?

BARBARA: Oh look, I don't understand it any more than you do. The inside of the Ship, suddenly finding ourselves here . . . even some of the things Doctor Foreman says. . .

IAN: That's not his name. Who is he? Doctor who? Perhaps if we knew his name we might have a clue to all this.

BARBARA: Look Ian, the point is, it's happened.

IAN: Yes it has, but it's impossible to accept. I know I'm here, but. . .

*(*SUSAN *returns.)*

SUSAN: I can't see him anywhere.

*(*BARBARA *detects a note of anxiety in* SUSAN*'s voice.)*

BARBARA: He can't be far away.

SUSAN: I've a feeling just now, as if we were being watched. Grandfather!

5. *ROCKY ENCLOSURE.*

(*THE DOCTOR is sitting on the ground, surrounded by his possessions. He has his back to* KAL. *THE DOCTOR gets up, lighting a pipe.* KAL *jumps down onto* THE DOCTOR, *who cries out.*)

6. *SAND DUNES.*

(*IAN, SUSAN and* BARBARA *all hear* THE DOCTOR*'s cry.*)

SUSAN: Grandfather!

IAN: Come on.

(*The three of them run in the direction of the sound.*)

7. *ROCKY ENCLOSURE.*

(*THE DOCTOR's bag and smashed Geiger counter lie on the ground.*)

IAN: Look!

SUSAN: What is it?

BARBARA: They're some of his things.

SUSAN: Oh, Grandfather, where are you?

IAN: Susan. Don't panic.

(SUSAN *is almost hysterical.*)

SUSAN: I must find him.

IAN: Susan.

SUSAN: I must see. . .

(SUSAN *climbs up a little way.*)

IAN: Well, be careful then.

(BARBARA *indicates the smashed remains of* THE DOCTOR*'s Geiger counter on the ground.*)

BARBARA: Ian. Look.

IAN: That's not much good anymore.

BARBARA: Well, maybe he saw something and . . . went off to investigate. . .

(IAN *picks up* THE DOCTOR*'s hat.*)

IAN: Leaving this?

BARBARA: Well, what do you think happened?

IAN: I don't know. Perhaps he was excited, and went off to investigate something as you suggest, but . . . he may have been taken.

(SUSAN *scrambles back down to the others.*)

SUSAN: I can't see him. I can't find him anywhere. There's not a sign of him.

IAN: Calm down, Susan.

BARBARA: Susan, don't worry.

> (SUSAN *bends down and picks up a notebook, and looks at them both.*)

BARBARA: What's the matter?

SUSAN: It's his notes. He'd never leave his notebook. It's too important to him. It's got the key-codes of all the machines in the Ship, and it's got notes of everywhere we've been to. Oh, something terrible has happened to him. I know it has. We must find him!

BARBARA: Susan. Susan. We'll find him, I promise you. He can't be far away.

IAN: What's on the other side of those rocks?

SUSAN: There's a line of trees. There's a gap in them. It might be a path on the other side.

IAN: All right. We'll try there first. Come on.

> (He puts the broken Geiger counter down on the sand. His hands come into contact with the sand.)

IAN: Strange. . .

BARBARA: What?

IAN: This sand. It's cold. It's nearly freezing.

8. *Campsite Outside Cave.*

(We see the OLD MOTHER *waiting there, while some of the tribeschildren play.)*

9. *Interior of Cave.*

HORG: Kal says where he comes from he's often seen men make fire.

ZA: Kal is a liar.

HORG: He says Orb will soon show him how it is done.

ZA: All his tribe died in the last cold. If he had not found us . . . he would have died too.

HUR: What else did he say?

HORG: He says Orb only shows the secret to the leader.

ZA: I am leader. Orb will show me.

(He continues talking to himself.)

ZA: I am the son of the great firemaker. But he does not show me how to put flames into the sticks. Kal comes. I do not kill him. . . I let him eat with us and sleep in our caves. I will have to spill some blood and make people bow to me.

(From outside the cave they hear a commotion. ZA *grabs his weapon and leaps up.)*

10. *Campsite Outside Cave.*

(KAL *has* THE DOCTOR *over his shoulder.* ZA *emerges from the cave, followed by others.* KAL *carries* THE DOCTOR *to a large stone and dumps him on it.*)

ZA: This is a strange creature.

KAL: Is Za, son of the firemaker, afraid of an old man?

ZA: No.

KAL: When will Za make fire come from his hands?

ZA: When Orb decides it.

KAL: Orb is for strong men. Orb has sent me this creature. To make fire come from his fingers. I have seen it. Inside he is full of fire. Smoke comes from his mouth.

ZA: As lies come out of yours.

(*He kneels by* THE DOCTOR. KAL *kneels on the other side of* THE DOCTOR, *so that both men face each other over* THE DOCTOR's *body.*)

ZA: He wears strange skins.

KAL: Za is afraid. There was a strange tree. The creature was in it. Za would have run away had he seen it.

(ZA *grabs* KAL *by the throat.* KAL *knocks* ZA's *hands away and he stands up and addresses the tribesmen.*)

KAL: When I saw fire come from his fingers, I remembered Za, son of the firemaker. And when the cold comes you will all die if you wait for Za to make fire for you. I, Kal, am a true leader. We fought like the tiger and the bear, my strength was too much for him. He lay down to sleep. But I, Kal, carried him here to make fire for you.

(*The tribe nod their approval.*)

ZA: Why do you listen to Kal?

HORG: Za has many good skins. He has forgotten what the cold is like.

ZA: Tomorrow I kill many bears. You all have warm skins.

HORG: I say tomorrow you will rub your hands together and hold them to the dry sticks and ask Orb to send you fire, and the bears will stay warm in their own skins.

(*There is a murmur of agreement at this.*)

ZA: What I say I will do, I will do!

KAL: Aaah! The firemaker is dead. You all carry dry sticks with you. Tonight I make them burn. I am leader.

HUR: The creature has opened his eyes.

THE DOCTOR: Where is my . . . where. . .

(KAL addresses the crowd.)

KAL: Do you want fire, or do you want to die in the cold?

TRIBE: Fire! Fire!

KAL: It is cold. The tiger comes to our caves again at night. Za will give you to the tiger. Za will give you to the cold. Za rubs his hands and waits for Orb to remember him. My creature can make fire come from his fingers. I have seen it. But I, Kal, brought him here. The creature is mine.

(He speaks to the tribe.)

ZA: Just an old man in strange skins. Kal has been with us too long. It is time he died.

(He advances on KAL with his stone axe. HORG, who is HUR's father, a man of some stature, steps between the two men.)

HORG: I say there is truth in both of you. Za speaks truth that fire cannot live in men, and Kal speaks the truth that we die without fire.

HUR: Will my father listen to a woman? If this old man can make fire come from his fingers, let us see it now.

ZA: I say what is to be done here. Not old men and women. . .

KAL: Za tries to talk like his father the firemaker. Za does not want to see fire made. But I, Kal, am not afraid of fire. I will make my creature make fire.

(THE DOCTOR _sits up, rubbing his head. He follows their conversation._)

ZA: I will take him to the Cave of Skulls, and he will tell me the secret.

(THE DOCTOR _is forced into action. He gets up and quickly moves to stand by_ HORG.)

THE DOCTOR: I can make fire for you. Let me go and I'll make all the fire you want. You don't have to be afraid of me. I'm an old man. How can an old man like me harm any of you?

ZA: What does he say?

HORG: Fire. He says he can make fire for us.

KAL: He makes it for me. But I give you fire. I am firemaker.

ZA: He will make it for me.

(THE DOCTOR _is searching desperately in his pockets. He mutters to himself._)

THE DOCTOR: My matches. Where are they?

ZA: What does he do now?

THE DOCTOR: I have none. Must get back to the Ship.

KAL: He is Kal's creature. He makes fire only for Kal.

THE DOCTOR: Take me back to my Ship, and I will make fire for you. All the fire you want.

(ZA angrily addresses KAL.)

ZA: This is more of your lies. The old man cannot make fire.

KAL: No. There was a tree. The creature came from in it. And the fire, it came out of his fingers.

ZA: You want to be strong like Za, son of the great firemaker.

(He addresses the crowd.)

ZA: You all heard him say that there would be fire. There is no fire. Za does not tell you lies. He does not say 'I will do this thing' and then not do it. He does not say 'I will make you warm' and then leave you to the dark. He does not say 'I will frighten away the tiger with fire' and then let him come to you in the dark. Do you want a liar for your chief?

TRIBE: No!

(KAL grabs THE DOCTOR and shakes him violently.)

KAL: Make fire. Make fire!!

HUR: You are trapped in your own lies, Kal.

(ZA mocks KAL.)

ZA: Look at the great chief who is afraid of nothing. Oh, great Kal, save us from the cold. Save us from the tiger.

(The crowd laugh at KAL. KAL suddenly grabs THE DOCTOR by his hands.)

KAL: Make fire. Make fire come from your fingers as I saw it today.

THE DOCTOR: I have no matches. I cannot make fire. I cannot make fire!

ZA: Let the old man die. And we'll watch the great Kal as he kills his strong enemy.

(ZA laughs at KAL. KAL grabs THE DOCTOR by the throat and points the knife-like stone at him.)

KAL: Make fire. Make fire or I kill you now.

ZA: And we will keep the great Kal to hunt for us. It is good to have someone to laugh at.

(KAL raises his knife high and is about to plunge it into THE DOCTOR. SUSAN and the others come into view. SUSAN screams. IAN struggles with KAL. ZA lifts an axe to kill IAN. BARBARA screams and struggles.)

THE DOCTOR: If he dies, there will be no fire.

(ZA *stops his axe in its downward stroke.* ZA *pushes* IAN *away.* KAL *reaches out to touch* BARBARA's *face.*)

OLD MOTHER: Kill her. Kill her.

(KAL *reaches for his knife.*)

ZA: Wait! We do not kill. . .

(*They struggle.*)

KAL: They are enemies.

ZA: When Orb gives fire back to the sky, let him look down on them. Then, that is when they die, and Orb will give us fire again.

(KAL *concedes.*)

ZA: Take them to the Cave of Skulls.

(SUSAN *struggles in vain.*)

SUSAN: No. No. Grandfather. No. No.

(*The four captives are hustled out.* KAL, *at the entrance to the cave, looks at* ZA *and then follows the others out.* HORG *starts to move to the entrance. He puts his hand on* HUR's *shoulder.* ZA *stops him.*)

ZA: The woman is mine.

HORG: My daughter is for the leader of the tribe.

ZA: Yes. The woman is mine.

HORG: I do not like what has happened.

ZA: Old men never like new things to happen.

HORG: I was a great leader of many men.

ZA: Many men. Yes. They all died when Orb left the sky and the great cold was on the ground. But Orb will give me fire again. To me, not to you. Just as you will give me Hur.

HUR: Za will be a strong leader of many men. If you give me to him, he will remember, and always give you meat.

(HORG *nods slowly and moves out of the cave.*)

OLD MOTHER: There were leaders before there was fire. Fire will kill us all in the end. You should have killed the four strangers. Kill them!

ZA: I have said we will wait until Orb shines again. Then they die.

11. INSIDE CAVE OF SKULLS (NIGHT).

(*The four travellers have been securely tied up by the tribe, their wrists bound together and their ankles. IAN is last to be tied. He falls to the ground and whispers to* BARBARA.)

IAN: Are you all right? Did they hurt you?

BARBARA: No. Ian, I'm frightened.

IAN: Try and hang on.

BARBARA: But how are we going to get out of this?

THE DOCTOR: We must use our cunning. I hope you can get yourself free, Chesterton. I can't. The stench. The stench. I'm sorry, it's all my fault. I'm desperately sorry.

SUSAN: Don't blame yourself, Grandfather.

THE DOCTOR: Look. Look at that. Look at it!

(He nods towards a pile of skulls.)

IAN: They're all the same. They've been split open.

Next Episode:
THE FOREST OF FEAR

THE FOREST OF FEAR

1. CAVE OF SKULLS (NIGHT).

THE DOCTOR: Oh, I'm sorry. I'm sorry, it's all my fault. I'm desperately sorry.

SUSAN: Oh, don't blame yourself, Grandfather.

THE DOCTOR: Look at those. Look at them.

(He is looking at a pile of skulls.)

IAN: Yes. They're all the same. They've been split wide open.

2. MAIN CAVE.

(The tribe is asleep. Slowly, the OLD MOTHER's head raises itself from the skins around her. Gradually, she eases herself out of the skins and makes her way cautiously over to ZA. Near to ZA's outflung hand is a sharp piece of stone which serves as his knife. She takes it in her hand, her face triumphant.)

> ### 3. *CAVE OF SKULLS.*
>
> *(IAN is desperately trying to cut BARBARA's bonds with a stone.)*

SUSAN: I've found another piece with a rough edge.

> *(She crawls over to IAN with difficulty, since she is also bound hand and foot and passes him the stone.)*

IAN: Oh, thank you.

> *(He tries unsuccessfully to use the stone.)*

IAN: It's no good. It keeps crumbling.

THE DOCTOR: Oh, it's hopeless. Hopeless. Even if we do get free. We shall never move that stone.

IAN: There's air coming in here from somewhere.

BARBARA: Yes, there is. I can feel it on my face.

IAN: It may only be a small opening. Don't count on it.

THE DOCTOR: You obviously are.

IAN: Of course I am. Any hope is better than none. Don't just lie there, criticising us. Do something. Help us all to get out of here!

> *(Again he tries to cut BARBARA's bonds.)*

IAN: Oh! This stone's no good.

(He throws it away in disgust.)

BARBARA: Don't give up, Ian. Please.

IAN: Oh, all right.

THE DOCTOR: Oh no. Don't waste time. Try those bones, they're sharper perhaps.

IAN: That's a good idea.

SUSAN: Oh, Grandfather. I knew you'd think of something.

THE DOCTOR: We must all take it in turns and try and cut his hands free.

IAN: Surely we should get the girls free. . .

THE DOCTOR: No, no. We've got to free you first, you're the strongest and you may have to defend us.

4. MAIN CAVE.

*(*HUR *wakes up and sees the* OLD MOTHER *with the knife in her hand leaving the cave.)*

5. OUTSIDE THE TWO CAVES.

(The OLD MOTHER *comes out of her cave, pauses at the Cave of Skulls, the entrance of which is blocked by a boulder, and then disappears into some bushes beyond.)*

6. *CAVE OF SKULLS.*

(THE DOCTOR *is now trying to sever* IAN'*s bonds.*)

THE DOCTOR: Oh, Susan. You have a go. My arms are tired.

SUSAN: All right.

THE DOCTOR: And don't think of failure.

BARBARA: What?

THE DOCTOR: Try and remember, if you can, how you and the others found your way here. Concentrate on that please.

BARBARA: Yes, yes. I'll try. . .

(*She realises suddenly what is happening.*)

BARBARA: You're trying to help me.

THE DOCTOR: Fear makes companions of all of us, Miss Wright.

BARBARA: I never once thought you were afraid.

THE DOCTOR: Fear is with all of us and always will be . . . just like that other sensation that lives with it.

BARBARA: What's that?

THE DOCTOR: Well, your companion referred to it. Hope. Hope, Miss Wright.

7. MAIN CAVE.

(HUR wakes ZA, and points to the empty skins where the OLD MOTHER had slept and then gestures to the cave mouth. ZA reaches for his knife, and realises it is no longer there. HUR indicates that someone has taken it. ZA picks up a stone axe – a piece of wood with a stone tied to the top – and they both leave the cave.)

8. CAVE OF SKULLS.

(BARBARA is now busily sawing away at IAN's bonds. SUSAN suddenly screams. A pile of branches against the cave wall moves and falls away to reveal the OLD MOTHER standing there, the knife of stone clutched firmly in her hand. She steps into the cave, the knife held out menacingly.)

OLD MOTHER: You will not make fire.

9. OUTSIDE THE TWO CAVES.

(We hear the sound of animal cries in the distance.)

ZA: Now tell me.

HUR: I saw the old woman take your knife.

ZA: Why did you let her? She is old. You could have held her.

HUR: Why did she take it?

ZA: She has gone into the forest.

HUR: No. She is going to kill the strangers.

ZA: Did she say this?

HUR: No. But she took your knife. She is afraid of fire.

ZA: You should have stopped her.

HUR: Kal was in the cave. Leaders are awake when others sleep. The strange tribe will not be able to show you how to make fire if the old woman kills them.

ZA: If I stop her from killing them . . . they will give fire to me and not to Kal.

(He goes to the blocked cave entrance.)

ZA: The old woman could not have gone into the cave. The great stone is still there. Why did you tell me this?

(He pushes HUR *who staggers and falls to the ground.)*

HUR: No. No. The old woman. . .

(She listens at the cave entrance.)

ZA: The old woman is talking to them.

10. CAVE OF SKULLS.

OLD MOTHER: I will set you free, if you will go away and not make fire. Fire will bring trouble and death to the tribe.

THE DOCTOR: There will be no fire.

(The OLD MOTHER *suddenly hears the sound of* ZA *and* HUR *trying to move the stone.)*

11. OUTSIDE THE CAVE OF SKULLS.

*(*ZA *and* HUR *are straining to move the boulder.)*

HUR: No. We cannot move the great stone.

ZA: The old woman is talking to them. I will move it.

12. CAVE OF SKULLS.

(The OLD MOTHER *has untied the travellers.)*

OLD MOTHER: Hurry, hurry. You must go across the top . . . and into the trees.

(She gestures towards the passage beyond the skulls.)

IAN: Yes.

(SUSAN *goes into the passage followed by* BARBARA, THE DOCTOR *and then* IAN. *The* OLD MOTHER *hurries to get after them but she is too late. The boulder rolls away and* ZA *and* HUR *rush into the cave.* ZA *grabs hold of the* OLD MOTHER.)

HUR: She has set them free.

OLD MOTHER: They would have made fire. They would have made fire.

(ZA *pushes the* OLD MOTHER *away and moves to the secret passage. She wraps her arms around him in order to delay him. He wrestles with her and then hurls her to the ground.*)

ZA: They have gone into the night.

HUR: They have taken fire with them.

ZA: The beasts will kill them. They will kill us if we follow.

(HUR *picks up the axe and gives it to* ZA.)

HUR: Now you are leader. You are as strong as the beasts. You will be stronger still when you know how fire is made. Stronger than Kal.

(ZA *looks at* HUR. *He enters the passage.*)

13. *FOREST.*

(SUSAN *and* BARBARA *run through the thick forest, branches whipping their faces.* IAN *follows.* THE DOCTOR *is lagging behind and is in obvious distress. He leans against the trunk of a tree, gasping for breath.*)

THE DOCTOR: Stop. Stop. Just a minute. Let me get my breath.

(IAN *comes back.* BARBARA *and* SUSAN *wait anxiously in the background.*)

IAN: We can't stop here.

THE DOCTOR: Just a moment.

IAN: Look we . . . we've got to go further on. . .

THE DOCTOR: I know. I know that. . . I must breathe. . . I must breathe.

IAN: Try! Try! . . . I shall have to carry you.

THE DOCTOR: Oh, there's no need for that. Don't be so childish. I'm not senile. Just let me get my breath for a moment.

SUSAN: Oh, Grandfather! Come on.

(THE DOCTOR *nods and with difficulty moves on.* SUSAN *takes his hand.*)

THE DOCTOR: Yes. I'm not so young, you know.

SUSAN: I know.

BARBARA: Are you sure this is the right way?

IAN: Yes, I think so.

BARBARA: I . . . I can't remember. I . . . I simply can't remember.

> (IAN *puts his arms round* BARBARA *to comfort her.*)

IAN: We're free, Barbara. Think about that. Free!

BARBARA: Yes.

> (BARBARA *nods in agreement and they move off to follow the others. An animal roars in the distance.*)

14. CLEARING IN FOREST.

> (SUSAN *and* THE DOCTOR *stop at the edge of the clearing.* BARBARA *and* IAN *join them.*)

SUSAN: I'm sure I remember this place. But we didn't come round it. We went across it.

BARBARA: Yes, there was a sort of trail.

IAN: If that's true we must be quite near the Ship.

> (IAN *looks at* THE DOCTOR.)

IAN: How are you feeling?

THE DOCTOR: I'm all right. Don't keep on looking upon me as the weakest link of the party.

(BARBARA *gives a small cry.*)

IAN: What's the matter?

BARBARA: I don't know. I saw something over there in the bushes.

THE DOCTOR: Oh, what nonsense!

BARBARA: The bushes moved. I saw them. I saw them! Oh, we're never going to get out of this awful place. Never, never, never. . .

(*She is weeping hysterically.* IAN *hugs her, and she buries her face in his shoulder.*)

SUSAN: What do you think it could have been, Grandfather. . .

THE DOCTOR: Oh, sheer nonsense, child. Imagination. . .

BARBARA: We'll die in this terrible place. . .

(*Her words are almost lost as she sobs.*)

IAN: No we won't. We're going to get back to the Ship, and then we'll be safe.

BARBARA: Oh, Ian. What's happening to us?

IAN: Look, Barbara. We got out of the cave didn't we?

(BARBARA *calms down as* IAN *talks to her.*)

SUSAN: I'm so cold.

THE DOCTOR: I'm hot, with all this exertion.

     (IAN *comes over to* THE DOCTOR *and* SUSAN.)

IAN: We'll rest for a couple of minutes.

SUSAN: Oh good. Is there any chance of them following us?

THE DOCTOR: I expect so.

IAN: Yes. That's why I don't want to stop here too long.

THE DOCTOR: Do you think I want to?

     (SUSAN *goes over to* BARBARA.)

IAN: No. We'll change the order. You and Susan go in front. Barbara and I'll bring up the rear. Susan seems to remember the way better than any of us.

THE DOCTOR: You seem to have elected yourself leader of this little party.

IAN: There isn't time to vote on it.

THE DOCTOR: Just so long as you understand that I won't follow your orders blindly.

IAN: If there were only two of us, you could find your own way back to the Ship.

THE DOCTOR: Aren't you a tiresome young man?

IAN: And you're a stubborn old man. But you'll lead – the girls in between – and I'll bring up the rear, because that's the safest way.

Barbara was probably right. I thought I heard something when we stopped back there.

THE DOCTOR: Oh, sheer imagination.

IAN: Why are you so confident about it?

THE DOCTOR: I won't allow myself to be frightened out of my wits by mere shadows, that's all.

IAN: All right.

(The four sit down together.)

15. FOREST.

(ZA and HUR arrive at the place where THE DOCTOR had to stop for breath.)

HUR: Look there. There is a branch broken.

(ZA crouches down on his haunches, peering at the moonlit ground.)

ZA: They have strange feet.

HUR: They wear skins on their feet.

ZA: There are marks here.

(HUR points to the ground.)

HUR: They've gone this way.

(An animal growls nearby. ZA and HUR look around fearfully.)

ZA: It was wrong to do this. We should not have followed them.

HUR: We cannot turn back now.

           (ZA *and* HUR *creep away,* ZA *holding his axe at the ready.*)

16. CLEARING IN FOREST.

IAN: I think we'd better get going. Doctor, will you lead?

           (THE DOCTOR *snaps impatiently at* IAN.)

THE DOCTOR: Yes, yes, yes, yes.

IAN: Come on, Barbara.

           (BARBARA *trips over something on the ground. She is looking straight at a newly-killed animal. She screams.*)

17. BUSHES.

           (BARBARA'*s scream reaches* ZA.)

IAN (*oov*): Barbara! Barbara!

ZA: They are near. That was one of the women.

18. CLEARING IN FOREST.

(IAN *is comforting* BARBARA. *The dead animal lies beside them.*)

SUSAN: It's an animal. . .

THE DOCTOR: This has just been killed. By a larger animal too. Quiet!

19. THE FOREST.

(*We see* ZA *and* HUR *creeping through the undergrowth.*)

20. CLEARING IN FOREST.

(IAN *listens. The others are alert.* BARBARA's *face shows clearly the strain, but she is quiet now, anticipating fresh terrors.*)

IAN: Shh, shh. That must be them. They've followed us. Quick. Quick . . . over there. . .

(*He hurries them behind some bushes. There is a moment's pause as the crashing of* ZA *and* HUR *gets nearer.* ZA *enters the clearing and stops.* HUR *follows and stands beside him. They look around the clearing.*)

21. BUSHES.

(The four are crouched in the bushes.)

IAN: Keep down, and not a sound.

22. CLEARING IN FOREST.

(ZA grasps HUR's shoulder. He looks about, and suddenly tenses, indicating to HUR a bush that is moving slightly.)

ZA: Wait. There is danger. I will go.

(HUR nods. ZA grasps his axe and advances into the clearing. There is a sudden throaty growl. ZA stops, freezing in his tracks, realising in an instant that this is not the humans for which he has been searching, but a far more dangerous adversary. The growl suddenly alters to a tremendous roar. ZA lifts his axe to defend himself, but is too late. HUR screams.)

23. BUSHES.

(HUR's scream echoes around them. BARBARA flinches.)

IAN: Quick, now's our chance. Let's get away . . . run!

(THE DOCTOR *and* SUSAN *scramble up
and start to move.* BARBARA *holds* IAN
back.)

BARBARA: Look. We can't just leave them. I don't care
what they've done.

IAN: Barbara. Barbara. Come on.

24. CLEARING IN FOREST.

(HUR, *kneeling beside the prostrate
body of* ZA. *She is bitterly anguished,
and is rocking slightly on her knees,
weeping.*)

25. BUSHES.

BARBARA: I think he's dead . . . there isn't any
danger. . . No.

(She runs off.)

IAN: Barbara, for heaven's sake!

BARBARA: No.

SUSAN: I'm going too.

THE DOCTOR: Susan. You stay here with me.

SUSAN: No, Grandfather. We can't leave them. . .

THE DOCTOR: We're going back to the Ship.

SUSAN: No. . .

(SUSAN *breaks free from his grip.*)

THE DOCTOR: What are you doing. . . They must be out of their minds.

26. CLEARING IN FOREST.

(HUR *doesn't know what to do with the blood-covered body of* ZA. *She looks up as* IAN *approaches.*)

HUR: Keep away. . .

IAN: Let me look at him. . .

HUR: No!

IAN: I am . . . your friend. You understand? . . . Friend. I want to help him.

(*He kneels beside* ZA.)

HUR: Friend?

IAN: I want water.

HUR: Water?

IAN: Go and fetch some water for his wounds.

HUR: Water is there.

BARBARA: Please show me.

(BARBARA *turns to* IAN.)

BARBARA: Give me your handkerchief.

(BARBARA *and* HUR *go for water.*
SUSAN *looks at* THE DOCTOR *as if
chastising him for trying to hold her
back. He lowers his eyes.*)

SUSAN: Is he all right?

IAN: I think so. He must have buried his axe-head in the animal.

(HUR *and* BARBARA *return with water.*)

IAN: Thank you.

(IAN *squeezes the water into* ZA's *wounds.*)

HUR: Water comes out of the skin.

IAN: Yes. I think most of this is the animal's blood.

SUSAN: Oh good.

BARBARA: There's a scar on the side of his head.

IAN: Well, we've lost our chance of getting away. . .

(*He looks at* BARBARA.)

IAN: Your flat must be littered with stray cats and dogs.

BARBARA: These are human beings, Ian. . .

IAN: Yes, I know.

(THE DOCTOR *emerges from the bushes.*)

THE DOCTOR:	What exactly do you think you're doing?
IAN:	Have you got any antiseptic in the Ship?
SUSAN:	Yes. Lots.
THE DOCTOR:	One minute ago we were trying desperately to get away from these savages. . .
IAN:	All right . . . now we're helping them. You're a doctor. Do something!
THE DOCTOR:	I'm not a doctor of medicine.
SUSAN:	Grandfather, we can make friends with them.
THE DOCTOR:	Oh, don't be ridiculous, child!
BARBARA:	Why? You treat everybody and everything as something less important than yourself.
THE DOCTOR:	You're trying to say that everything you do is reasonable, and everything I do is inhuman. Well, I am afraid your judgement's at fault, Miss Wright, not mine. Haven't you realised if these two people can follow us, the whole tribe might descend upon us at any moment.
HUR:	The tribe is asleep.
THE DOCTOR:	And what about the old woman who cut our bonds? Hmm? You understand. Hmm?

(*There is a moment's pause.* IAN *sees from* HUR'*s expression that she had forgotten the* OLD MOTHER.)

IAN: He's right. We're too exposed here. We'll make a stretcher and carry him.

THE DOCTOR: You're not going to take him back to the Ship?

(IAN ignores him.)

IAN: Take your coat off, Barbara. Susan, try and find me two poles. Long ones. Fairly straight.

BARBARA: The old woman won't give us away. She helped.

THE DOCTOR: You think so? These people have logic and reason, have they? Can't you see their minds change as rapidly as night and day? She's probably telling the whole tribe at this very moment.

27. CAVE OF SKULLS.

(The OLD MOTHER, still dazed on the ground, begins to recover her senses. She suddenly realises that she is not alone.)

KAL: The creatures? Where? Where?

OLD MOTHER: Gone.

KAL: The great stone. They could not move it.

OLD MOTHER: Za moved it.

KAL: Za has gone with them? Tell me!

OLD MOTHER: Za and Hur went after them.

KAL: There were skins around their hands and their feet. They could not move. Za helped them get free. They have gone with Za, to show him fire.

OLD MOTHER: They won't make fire. There won't be fire anymore.

KAL: Old woman. You helped them.

(KAL's hand reaches for the stone knife tucked into his waistband, and raises it.)

28. CLEARING IN FOREST.

(IAN has now constructed a rough stretcher.)

IAN: It's not going to work like this. What can we do?

(THE DOCTOR looks on from a distance. HUR notices SUSAN tending ZA.)

HUR: He is mine!

SUSAN: I was only trying to help.

IAN: She doesn't understand, Susan. She's jealous of you.

HUR: I do not understand what you are doing. You are like . . . like a mother with a child. Why do you not kill?

(IAN *talks to* BARBARA.)

IAN: How can we explain to her? She doesn't understand kindness . . . friendship.

(BARBARA *talks to* HUR.)

BARBARA: We will make him well again. We will teach you how to make fire. In return, you show us the way back to . . . to our cave.

(ZA *by now has recovered consciousness.*)

ZA: Listen to them. They do not kill.

IAN: Come on, let's get on with this stretcher. Let's try the sleeves inside. That's it.

ZA: Water.

(HUR *goes to fetch some more water.*)

IAN: How about giving us a hand, Doctor?

(THE DOCTOR *turns his back on* IAN.)

SUSAN: He's always like this if he doesn't get his own way.

BARBARA: Well, the old woman won't give us away . . . and now that we've got these two on our side . . . we should get back to the Ship.

SUSAN: Yes.

(THE DOCTOR *bends over by* ZA. *He picks up a large stone. Suddenly, a hand grips his wrist.* IAN *looks closely at* THE DOCTOR.)

THE DOCTOR: Let go of me.

IAN: What are you doing?

THE DOCTOR: Well . . . I was going to get him to draw our way back to the TARDIS.

IAN: We've been too long as it is. Is the stretcher ready?

BARBARA: Yes.

IAN: All right. You take one end of it.

THE DOCTOR: You don't expect me to carry him, do you?

IAN: Do you want the women to do the job for you?

THE DOCTOR: Oh, very well.

IAN: Right. Now. Move him over very carefully. Now . . . back again . . . gently . . . good. Right, now Susan, you get in front with her.

29. *OUTSIDE MAIN CAVE.*

(*The tribe is awake and talking loudly amongst themselves.*)

KAL: They have gone. Za and Hur have gone with them. We must go after them.

HORG: Hur would not help them to get away.

KAL: She has gone with them.

HORG: The old woman sleeps in the cave too, and she has gone.

KAL: The old woman is in the Cave of Skulls.

HORG: Hur would not go with them.

KAL: Ask the old woman. She will tell what is done.

> _30. TRAIL THROUGH FOREST._
>
> _(The group is slowly moving down the trail.)_

> _31. CAVE OF SKULLS._
>
> _(HORG, KAL and the others enter the cave. The OLD MOTHER is sitting.)_

KAL: She will tell.

> _(KAL pushes the OLD MOTHER and she falls over. HORG touches her, and realises that she is dead.)_

KAL: My eyes tell me what has happened . . . as they do when I sleep and I see things. Za and Hur came to free them and find the way to make fire. The old woman saw them. Za killed the old woman.

HORG: The old woman is dead. It must have been as your eyes said it was.

KAL: Za has gone with them . . . taking them to their cave. Za takes away fire. Now I, Kal, lead.

(KAL *goes to the mouth of the cave. The rest move after him. He is now leader.*)

32. *EDGE OF THE FOREST.*

IAN: Hold the branches back, Susan.

(*As* SUSAN *pulls the branches back, we see the police box standing a short way from the edge of the bushes.*)

SUSAN: The TARDIS. There's the TARDIS.

(*Without warning, tribesmen suddenly emerge from hiding, and advance towards the travellers.*)

IAN: Back. Come back.

(*It is too late.* KAL *and some other tribesmen are behind them. They are surrounded.* SUSAN *screams.*)

Next Episode:
THE FIREMAKER

EPISODE FOUR

THE FIREMAKER

1. EDGE OF THE FOREST (NIGHT).

IAN: Back. Get back.

(The tribesmen appear from their hiding places.)

2. OUTSIDE THE CAVES.

HORG: They are coming.

(The four travellers carrying ZA on their home-made stretcher enter, surrounded by tribesmen.)

KAL: Za and the woman went with them. I, Kal, stopped them.

HUR: They saved Za from death near the stream.

KAL: They set them free from the Cave of Skulls and went with them.

HUR: The old woman cut them free.

KAL: Za is so weak the woman speaks for him.

HUR: It was the old woman. She showed them a new way out of the Cave of Skulls.

KAL: The old woman does not speak. She does not say she did this or did that. The old woman is dead.

(The tribespeople mutter.)

KAL: Za killed the old woman.

HUR: No.

KAL: Za killed the old woman with his knife.

(He bends over ZA and takes the knife, which is stuck in the folds of ZA's garment.)

KAL: Here. Here is the knife he killed her with.

(He holds the knife up.)

THE DOCTOR: This knife has no blood on it.

(There is no reaction.)

THE DOCTOR: I said this knife has no blood on it.

(KAL recovers from his momentary confusion.)

KAL: It is a bad knife.

(He drops it.)

KAL: It does not show the things it does.

THE DOCTOR: It is a finer knife than yours.

KAL: I, Kal, say it is a bad knife.

THE DOCTOR: This knife can cut and stab. I have never seen a better knife.

KAL: I will show you one.

(He pulls a knife from his clothes. It is covered with blood.)

THE DOCTOR: This knife shows what it has done. There is blood on it.

(There is a gasp from the tribespeople, as THE DOCTOR *shows the knife to them.)*

THE DOCTOR: Who killed the old woman?

ZA: I did not kill her.

*(*THE DOCTOR *turns to* KAL.*)*

THE DOCTOR: You killed the old woman.

(The tribespeople murmur.)

KAL: Yes! She set them free. She set them free. She did this. I, Kal, killed her.

*(*THE DOCTOR *addresses the tribespeople.)*

THE DOCTOR: Is this your strong leader? One who kills your old women? He is a bad leader. He will kill you all.

> (THE DOCTOR *bends down and picks up a small rock. He whispers urgently to* IAN.)

THE DOCTOR: Follow my example. . .

> (*To the tribe.*)

THE DOCTOR: Drive him out. . . Drive him out.

> (*He throws the stone at* KAL.)

IAN: Yes, drive him out. He killed the old woman.

> (IAN *also throws stones at* KAL. KAL *is surprised at this. The stones do not really harm him, but do startle him. He lunges into the tribe, but they push him away, their stones driving him away.*)

TRIBE: Drive him out.

> (IAN *goes over to* ZA.)

IAN: Remember, Kal is not stronger than the whole tribe.

ZA: Kal is no longer one of this tribe. We will watch for him. We will all fight Kal if he comes back. We will watch for him.

ZA: Take them to the Cave of Skulls.

IAN: Take us back to the desert and we will make fire for you.

ZA: The great stone will close one place, and you will stand by another I will show you. Take them.

THE DOCTOR: Don't struggle.

(The four travellers are escorted into the Cave of Skulls.)

ZA: They are inside the cave. If you see them come out . . . kill them.

3. BUSH NEAR THE CAVE OF SKULLS.

(KAL parts the bush and peers through. His face is watchful. He is determined to get his revenge.)

4. INSIDE THE CAVE OF SKULLS.

(The four prisoners are examining the inside of the cave. SUSAN sees the OLD MOTHER lying dead on the floor and retches. BARBARA comforts her.)

THE DOCTOR: This place is evil.

(IAN discovers that the secret entrance to the cave has been closed off.)

5. OUTSIDE THE CAVE OF SKULLS.

ZA: Tell me what happened after I fought the beast in the forest.

HUR: You were stronger than the beast. It took away your axe . . . in its head. You lay on the earth. I believed you were dead.

ZA: Tell me what they did.

HUR: The young man of their tribe came towards you, but he did not kill. He told me his name.

ZA: Name?

HUR: His name is Friend.

ZA: They come from the other side of the mountains.

HUR: Nothing lives there.

ZA: There are other tribes there. This new tribe must come from there. Tell me more of what happened.

HUR: I did not understand them. Their hands moved slowly, and their faces were not fierce. It was like a mother guarding her baby.

ZA: They are a new tribe. Not like us. Not like Kal. The young one whose name is Friend spoke to me.

HUR: Do you remember it?

ZA: He said 'Kal is not stronger than the whole tribe'.

HUR: I do not understand.

ZA: The whole tribe drove Kal away with the stones. The whole tribe can collect more fruit than one. The whole tribe can kill a beast, where one of the tribe would die.

HUR: Do you think they come from Orb?

ZA: No. They are a tribe who know how fire is made, but they do not want to tell us.

HUR: Then you will not kill them?

ZA: Horg says the leader must know how fire is made. I do not want to be driven into the forest like Kal. I must make fire. Or they must die, as the old men say. I will speak with them. I must hear more things to remember. The leader would have things to remember.

6. *INSIDE THE CAVE OF SKULLS (DAY).*

(IAN *has taken the lace from one of his shoes and has just finished making a bow with the lace and a small willowy branch. In the lace is wrapped another piece of wood.*)

SUSAN: I think this is what you want, Mr. Chesterton.

(SUSAN *brings* IAN *a flat round stone with a hollow in the centre of it.*)

BARBARA: Here are some leaves and some dead grass.

IAN: Thank you. Yes, well spread them round the hole. Don't put them inside. I hope this is going to work. No, spread them round a bit more. Yes, that's it.

> (IAN *starts to rub the wood up and down the bow, in an effort to make fire.* BARBARA *packs the grass and leaves around it.*)

7. OUTSIDE THE CAVE OF SKULLS.

(ZA and a tribesman.)

ZA: I will speak with them. You wait here.

> (*The tribesman nods.* ZA *enters the hidden passage into the cave. The camera pulls back to reveal* KAL *watching from above.*)

8. INSIDE THE CAVE OF SKULLS.

SUSAN: I can smell something.

BARBARA: Yes, so can I.

SUSAN: It's burning. It's burning.

IAN: It's a long way off yet.

> (*He grits his teeth and perseveres.*)

ZA: What is this?

(They swing round and see ZA.*)*

THE DOCTOR: We are making fire.

*(*ZA *comes nearer and looks down at* IAN.*)*

ZA: You are called Friend?

IAN: Yes.

*(*IAN *looks up in surprise and stops.)*

THE DOCTOR: Don't stop.

ZA: Hur said you were called Friend. I am Za. You are the leader of your tribe.

*(*IAN *looks at* ZA, *and then at* THE DOCTOR.*)*

IAN: No. He is our leader.

*(*IAN *looks at* SUSAN, *who smiles and looks at* ZA.*)*

SUSAN: Are you going to set us free?

ZA: The tribe say you are from Orb, and that when you are returned to him on the stone of death, we will have fire again.

BARBARA: But that's not true.

ZA: I think you are from the other side of the mountains. If you show me how to make fire, I will take you back to the foot of the mountains. If you do not show me, I cannot stop you dying on the old stone.

IAN: Put some more leaves and grass round it. I think it's beginning to work.

THE DOCTOR: Do you understand? We are making fire, for you.

ZA: I am watching.

IAN: The whole tribe should be watching. Everyone should know how to make fire.

ZA: Everyone cannot be leader.

IAN: No, that's perfectly true. But in our tribe the firemaker is the least important man.

ZA: I do not believe it.

THE DOCTOR: He is the least important, because we can all make fire.

(SUSAN whispers under her breath.)

SUSAN: I hope he doesn't make Grandfather prove that.

(A little plume of smoke rises.)

IAN: Look! I think it's beginning to work. Susan! Barbara! Blow gently.

(SUSAN and BARBARA start to blow. SUSAN puts on some more leaves. The smoke is rising more thickly now. Suddenly, there is a crackling sound,

and a small flame. Then another. Then the whole pile is burning. IAN *stops 'sawing', puts away the bow and starts adding little twigs and branches until a blaze begins to build up.)*

SUSAN: You've done it!

IAN: Yes.

           *(*ZA *stares   at   the   flames   in wonderment.)*

ZA: Fire. Fire.

9. *INSIDE THE MAIN CAVE.*

*(*HORG *and some of the other tribes-people are grouped there.* HUR *sits near the entrance, listening.)*

HORG: Orb strikes the old stone, and Za does not bring them out. We have no meat and no fruit from the trees and no roots. Za is no leader.

HUR: Za would kill you if he could hear you. He is talking now with them in the Cave of Skulls. You should lie on the old stone 'til your blood runs into the earth.

HORG: Za is letting them go away. Just as the old woman set them free.

HUR: Za told one of us to watch and guard them until he came out of the Cave of Skulls.

10. OUTSIDE THE CAVE OF SKULLS.

(The guard is waiting outside the cave. Suddenly, two hands appear from behind and strangle him. The guard goes limp.)

11. INSIDE THE CAVE OF SKULLS.

(KAL enters.)

SUSAN: Look!

(They all spin around. KAL crouches down as ZA springs to his feet, clutching for his knife. ZA and KAL circle around the fire as the travellers look on, horrified. The two cavemen fight, and eventually ZA wins, killing KAL. Suddenly there is the sound of shouting from outside the cave.)

12. OUTSIDE THE TWO CAVES.

(HUR is struggling with a tribesman who is holding her arms behind her. HORG is leading the tribe out of the main cave.)

HORG: Orb is above us and there is no fire. Bring them out from the Cave of Skulls. And Za as well.

13. INSIDE THE CAVE OF SKULLS.

(IAN *pulls a long piece of wood from the fire, its end ablaze like a torch. He hands it to* ZA.)

IAN: Take this. Show it to your tribe.

(ZA *takes it.*)

ZA: You stay here.

(*Outside the cave, the chanting grows louder.*)

IAN: We will come with you. . .

ZA: No! Stay here.

IAN: I will come with you.

(ZA *threatens* IAN *with the blazing torch.* THE DOCTOR *grasps* IAN *to prevent him following.*)

THE DOCTOR: Give him a chance. Give him a chance. Let him show the tribe fire, establish himself as leader, then he'll let us go.

IAN: But we ought to go with him now.

14. OUTSIDE THE TWO CAVES.

(ZA *runs out of the cave. There is*

> *immediate silence from the tribe.* ZA
> *advances, holding the torch aloft.)*

ZA: Fire.

TRIBE: Fire.

ZA: Kal is dead. I give you fire. I am leader!

> (HORG *looks up at the flames and nods.*
> *He holds his hands out to the flames.)*

HORG: Yes.

> *(The tribespeople cheer.)*

ZA: We will give food and water to the new tribe in the Cave of Skulls.

HORG: There is no meat.

ZA: I will go into the forest and get meat.

HORG: Yes. I remember how the meat and fire joined together.

ZA: Good. Watch the new tribe. They must be here when I return.

15. INSIDE THE CAVE OF SKULLS.

IAN: It didn't work. They're going to keep us here.

> (HUR *enters. She comes over to the*
> *travellers and puts some food down by*
> *the fire.)*

IAN: Why are you keeping us here?

HUR: Za has gone into the forest to find meat. There will be more food later.

BARBARA: But why can't we go outside?

SUSAN: Please let us go. It's terrible in here.

HUR: Za is leader.

SUSAN: We helped you. We gave you fire.

HUR: Yes, we have fire now.

(HUR *leaves the cave.*)

IAN: Yes. I was the fool who gave it to you. Why didn't I wait?

BARBARA: Well at least we're alive. We wouldn't be if we hadn't given them fire.

16. *OUTSIDE THE TWO CAVES (EVENING).*

(It is some hours later. It is already getting dark. The fire is roaring and the tribespeople are sitting round it, arms stretched towards the flames.)

17. *INSIDE THE CAVE OF SKULLS (NIGHT).*

(IAN *is asleep.* BARBARA *shakes him.*)

BARBARA: Ian.

IAN: Huh. . .

(IAN *sits up.*)

SUSAN: They brought us some meat.

BARBARA: And the Doctor found a stone with a hole in it, and they've filled it with water.

IAN: All the comforts of home.

(ZA *enters.*)

ZA: The animal was hard to kill.

(*The travellers ignore him.*)

ZA: The meat on it is good.

(*Again they ignore him.*)

ZA: They have brought you fruit, and water has been put into a stone.

(*Silence.*)

ZA: Is this the stone?

(*Silence.* ZA *is puzzled by their silence. He bends down and touches the stone.*)

ZA: Has anyone hurt you?

THE DOCTOR: When are you going to let us go? Hmm?

ZA: You will stay here. I have the meat and I have the stick and the piece of skin. I can make fire now. Your tribe and my tribe will join together.

IAN: We don't want to stay here.

ZA: Why? There is no better place the other side of the mountains. Do not try to leave here.

(He leaves the cave.)

THE DOCTOR: If only we could find some way of taking the fire away from them: scaring them . . . somehow.

(SUSAN walks across the cave carrying a burning torch, and puts a skull on top of it. The fire glows through the empty eye-sockets.)

SUSAN: Hey, Grandfather, look . . . it's almost alive!

IAN: Not alive, Susan . . . almost . . . dead! We're going to make four torches. We'll find the sticks and we'll use the fat from the meat. And then. . .

SUSAN: And then. . . ?

IAN: And then to all intents and purposes, we're going to die.

18. Outside the Caves.

(The tribe is seated around the fire.)

19. Inside the Cave of Skulls.

(The four travellers are crouched down in the shadows near the entrance to the cave.)

IAN: When I give the sign. . .

(HUR enters, and stops in terror when she sees four skulls on sticks, fire issuing from their eyes, noses and even their mouths. Other tribespeople have entered and moan in terror, kneeling down before the skulls.)

SUSAN: What are they all kneeling for?

(BARBARA puts her hand over SUSAN's mouth. IAN and the other three gradually edge their way around the kneeling tribe and creep out. IAN is the last to go.)

20. Outside the Caves.

(We see the four running past the blazing fire and away.)

21. INSIDE THE CAVE OF SKULLS.

(The tribespeople are still cowering in terror.)

22. FOREST.

(The four travellers flee through the undergrowth.)

23. INSIDE THE CAVE OF SKULLS.

(One of the torches and its skull falls over.)

ZA: Look! It is nothing but fire, and the bones of the dead. They have gone! While we look at their fire, they have gone!

HUR: Into the night. The dark will hide them.

(ZA looks at the fire and picks up a blazing stick.)

ZA: With fire it is day.

(ZA makes for the entrance.)

24. FOREST.

(The travellers run along. BARBARA trips over and is helped to her feet by IAN.)

25. *OUTSIDE THE CAVES.*

(The tribesmen, led by ZA*, stream out of the Cave of Skulls and run past the fire.)*

26. *FOREST.*

(The four travellers run through the forest, chased by the tribesmen, ZA *at their head. At last they reach the TARDIS and rush inside, shutting the door behind them.)*

27. *INSIDE THE TARDIS.*

*(*BARBARA *and* SUSAN *rush over to the console.)*

IAN:　　　　Come on, Doctor. Get us off. Get us off!

THE DOCTOR:　Yes. Yes. Yes.

(He rushes over to the console and operates some controls. The central column starts to rise, accompanied by the sound of dematerialization.)

28. *OUTSIDE THE TARDIS.*

(The tribespeople throw spears at the police box. As they do so, it dematerializes with a groaning sound. They stare in amazement.)

29. INSIDE THE TARDIS.

(THE DOCTOR *is staring at the controls, his hands occasionally going out to a switch.*)

THE DOCTOR: Yes, it's matching up.

SUSAN: We're beginning to land.

THE DOCTOR: Oh, how I wish. . .

IAN: Have you taken us back to our own time?

THE DOCTOR: You know I can't do that. Please be reasonable.

IAN: What?

BARBARA: Please . . . you must take us back . . . you must.

(THE DOCTOR *indicates the console.*)

THE DOCTOR: You see, this isn't operating properly. Or rather the code is still a secret. Feed it with the right data, precise information to a second at the beginning of a journey, and then we can fix a destination. But I have no data at my disposal.

BARBARA: Are you saying that you don't know how to work this thing?

THE DOCTOR: Oh, of course I can't. I'm not a miracle worker.

SUSAN: You can't blame Grandfather. We left the other place too quickly, that's all.

(The sounds of the TARDIS in flight begin to run down.)

IAN: Just a minute. Did you try and take us back to our own time?

THE DOCTOR: Well, I got you away from that other time, didn't I?

IAN: That isn't what I asked you.

THE DOCTOR: It's the only way I can answer you, young man.

(The TARDIS stops. Only the hum of the control room remains.)

THE DOCTOR: Now. Now we shall see.

(He presses a switch and looks at the scanner screen. We see a strange, alien forest.)

THE DOCTOR: It could be anywhere. Dear, dear, dear, dear. It's no help to us at all. Well, I suggest before we go outside and explore, let us clean ourselves up.

SUSAN: Yes.

THE DOCTOR: Now what does the radiation read, Susan?

SUSAN: It's reading normal, Grandfather.

(As they leave the console, the meter's needle rises steadily towards the danger point. The meter begins to flash once the danger point is passed.)

Next Episode:
THE DEAD PLANET*

* This was the first episode of the next story, which featured the introduction of the Daleks.

DOCTOR WHO PORTFOLIO

First in a series of portfolios featuring the universally popular BBC TV character, Doctor Who. This portfolio consists of five full colour prints, 16½ x 11¾in, by well known fantasy illustrator Chris Achilleos.

The titles of the prints are:

The Genesis of the Daleks (*BBC transmission 8/3/75 — 12/4/75.*) The evil Davros, creator of the Daleks, with an inset portrait of Tom Baker as The Doctor.

The Web of Fear (*BBC transmission 3/2/68 — 9/3/68*). The Doctor, as played by Patrick Troughton, looks on while a Yeti surrounds the figure of Sgt. Arnold with a deathly forcefield.

The Three Doctors (*BBC transmission 30/12/72 — 20/1/73*). Featuring the first three Doctors as portrayed by William Hartnell, Patrick Troughton and Jon Pertwee under the control of renegade Time Lord, Omega.

Invasion of the Dinosaurs (*BBC transmission 12/1/74 — 16/2/74*). Savage dinosaurs attack London and The Doctor, played by Jon Pertwee.

Tom Baker The Fourth Doctor Who, 1974 — 1981.

The plates are taken from the original artwork and printed on high quality art paper suitable for framing.

£3.99

STAR TREK NOVELS

These are original novels by new and established Science Fiction authors, featuring characters from the TV series.

1: CHAIN OF ATTACK by Gene De Weese.   **£2.95**
The Enterprise is caught up in a deadly interstellar conflict.

2: DEEP DOMAIN by Howard Weinstein.   **£2.95**
Spock and Chekov go missing on the watery planet of Akkalla.

3: DREAMS OF THE RAVEN by Carmen Carter.   **£2.95**
The Enterprise and Dr. McCoy are crippled in a mysterious alien attack.

4: THE ROMULAN WAY by Diane Duane and Peter Morwood.   **£2.95**
An insider's report from deep within the stronghold of the Romulan Empire.

5: HOW MUCH FOR JUST THE PLANET? by John M. Ford.   **£2.95**
On Direidi is the galaxy's greatest ever fortune in Dilithium crystals.

STAR TREK GIANT NOVELS

Epic stories that expand the *STAR TREK* universe.

STRANGERS FROM THE SKY by Margaret Wander Bonanno.   **£3.95**
Admiral James T. Kirk is tormented by dreams of an alternate reality.

STAR TREK LARGE FORMAT BOOKS

MR. SCOTT'S GUIDE TO THE ENTERPRISE by Shane Johnson.   **£6.95**
From the logbooks of Chief Engineer Montgomery Scott, an accurate, in-depth look at the USS Enterprise.

THE *STAR TREK* COMPENDIUM by Allan Asherman.   **£7.95**
A complete reference guide to the TV series, animated shows and *STAR TREK* films.

DON'T PANIC
The Official HITCH-HIKER'S GUIDE TO THE GALAXY Companion by Neil Gaiman.

Neil Gaiman tells the story of the Earthly existence of THE HITCH-HIKER'S GUIDE TO THE GALAXY, as radio series, books, television series, theatre productions, records, film, computer game and towel, and tells you everything you ever wanted to know about the life and times of Douglas Adams.

"It's all devastatingly true — except the bits that are lies." **—Douglas Adams**

£3.95